THE INVESTORS' ADVOCATE

Practical Counsel for Successful Investing

 FriesenPress

One Printers Way
Altona, MB R0G 0B0
Canada

www.friesenpress.com

ISBN
978-1-03-918095-6 (Hardcover)
978-1-03-918094-9 (Paperback)
978-1-03-918096-3 (eBook)

1. Business & Economics, Personal Finance, Investing

Distributed to the trade by The Ingram Book Company

To Dr. Vernon Krause, M.D., F.R.C.P.,
physician extraordinaire, friend and mentor.
With gratitude for your encouragement,
caring support and humanity.

TABLE OF CONTENTS

DISCLAIMER

The content of this book should not be misunderstood, misconstrued, or assumed in any way to constitute investment advice. It is provided as thinking advice. Nothing in this book or the references made within its contents is a recommendation to buy or sell any investment products or to make any investment. Nothing herein shall constitute an offer to buy or sell securities or the solicitation of any offer to buy or sell securities. Such actions may only be made upon presentation and delivery of an offering memorandum, prospectus, or other documentation in compliance with securities regulations.

The investment themes, philosophies, policies, and processes reflected in the subject matter of this book, or the references made by those contents represent simplified examples of the author's investment practices in the past. They are not the actual processes, policies, or philosophies employed by the author. That past practice differed significantly from the presentations here, in that they were more complex and tailored to individual investors' unique objectives. What is presented here is designed not for investment practice, as that cannot be done prudently without regard to the individual context of an investor's objectives.

The purpose of this book is not to advise, solicit, buy, or sell securities. This book is a tool for thinking about making investment decisions; specifically, the rational development of a fundamental framework for making investment decisions and the implementation of a process of due diligence through which the investor can protect that decision framework from being eroded by the investor's own emotions.

While the information contained in this book is believed to be accurate, errors and omissions excepted, the author makes no express or implied warranty as to the completeness or accuracy of the contents. As a result, the author cannot and will not accept any responsibility for errors, omissions, or inaccuracies appearing in this book. Neither will the author accept responsibility for any misinterpretations resulting from a reader's application of the concepts within this book.

By continuing to read this book, the reader expressly agrees to the release of the author from any liability related to their subsequent actions.

The content in this book is not intended be a substitute for, replace of, or to constitute professional, legal or investment advice. The materials contained in this book are intended to assist individuals in their investing efforts through being able to improve their thought process in formulating investment decisions. The creators of the materials shall not be held responsible for any claims or damages whatsoever relating to the results of their efforts directly or indirectly. Investing entails risks of loss, including loss of both capital and income, and those risks are entirely your own as the reader of this book.

Individuals who read this book expecting to make quick profit in the stock market are cautioned that they will likely be disappointed. The stock market often serves as the means for transferring wealth from those with short time horizons to patient investors with longer time horizons.

At the time of writing this book, there has been a 4-decade trend of declining interest rates which has served to expand asset values substantially. Should interest rates rise, it is likely that asset values will generally decline. That is but one of many risks investors face which are beyond the scope of this book and why it is recommended that readers seek competent professional advice before making investment decisions.

PROLOGUE

For the great majority of investors, the stock market represents a triumph of hope over experience. A wide continuity of studies over long periods from differing sources continue to show that the vast majority of investors underperform the markets. It is the fundamental precept of this book that this need not be the case. If the investor can think in a rational manner that protects them from their own emotions and the influence of the crowd of the investing public, then it is possible to achieve better relative outcomes than history shows to be the norm. If the biggest obstacle to investing success is the investor's own emotions, then the solution may reside in the use of process to frame the investors thinking.

That change in thinking about investing is the focus of this book.

If you want to teach people a new way of thinking, don't bother trying to teach them. Instead, give them a tool, the use of which will lead to new ways of thinking.

—Buckminster Fuller

"No great improvements in the lot of mankind are possible, until a great change takes place in the fundamental constitution of their modes of thought."

—John Stuart Mill, 1806-1873

INTRODUCTION

This book is written to help you be more successful in your investing and make more money over time. This was the focus of most of my career. I am retired now. Among the adjustments that one makes when retiring is adapting to a new routine and purpose. While still working, my focus was on helping individual clients meet their financial goals. But my clients are now well served by my successor. No longer being in a role focused on helping people to create value left a void.

Initially, the plan was to work part-time as a consultant to help investors review their investments—that is, to provide independent due diligence—so they would know that they were in competent hands with their financial advisor. Where they found they were not, they would have a clear path to address the issues.

It was clear that this would, in a short time, become a full-time endeavor that would replace retirement. Even with the ability to have a meaningful impact, the constraints of serving individual investors one-to-one meant I would only be able to help a small number of people.

Hence this book.

Who This Book is For

This book is intended to support those who are interested in investment success: individual investors, the investment professionals who advise them, and the investment firms that employ those investment professionals.

If you are an individual investor, you need to be aware that the intention to build wealth through investing often represents a triumph of hope over experience. As an investor, your emotions are the single biggest hurdle you face. Using the process in this book, instead of emotions, to make investment decisions is the single most important step you can take towards being a successful investor.

If you are an investment professional, you know that being able to articulate your own value proposition to clients and prospects is a key factor to success. This book provides a means for you to think differently about managing investments. This differential in thinking will build a sound intellectual framework for investment decisions that will enable you as a **fiduciary** to supply the emotional discipline to clients that is often in short supply when most needed.

If you are part of an investment firm, this book is one more way to help your clients and employees succeed. It can be used both as a business development asset and as an added benefit to your clients to show your appreciation for their patronage.

The intended audience for this book is quite narrow. Implementing the process that it describes, while quite simple in concept, does require diligent effort. That is why it is recommended that if you are an individual investor, you engage with professionals possessing the required expertise.

Individual personality traits of those who will benefit the most from the content of this book are the same character traits that the legendary Warren Buffett, CEO of Berkshire Hathaway, seeks in the management of his investments: *energy, intelligence, and character.*

Why energy? Effort is required to be a successful investor. This book comes with a standard advisory that "some assembly is required." It will be needed to write a Statement of Investment Objectives; develop a formal written Financial Plan (FP); and design and implement an Investment Policy Statement (IPS) to guide the execution of a sound framework for making investment decisions to realize your investment objectives.

Why intelligence? Modest intellect, rather than genius, will be required to personalize the provided tools into what works for you. The concepts herein are not of my creation but are an assembly of the work of others that collectively, are generally little known, and even less, properly understood. Thankfully, the math required for implementation is relatively simple. It does not require a genius IQ, inside information, or unusual insight. What is required is the ability to incorporate the tools contained in this book into a personalized framework for making investment decisions. This will form the basis of your Investment Policy Statement. This need not be complicated. For example, David Chilton in his book *The Wealthy Barber Returns*, succinctly describes one of the best examples he has seen of an individual's financial plan and investment policy in one page of text and applauds it for being simple and "nothin' fancy."[1]

> *Simplicity is the ultimate sophistication.*
> —Attributed to Leonardo da Vinci

Why character? Temperament is a key part of successful investing. The right temperament will enable you to make decisions with clear, independent, and rational reasoning. That reasoning is fundamental to being able to identify opportunities that others may overlook and to avoid risks that are created by

---

1   *The Wealthy Barber Returns*, David Chilton, 2011, pp. 223–224

the herd behaviors of market participants that follow popular themes carried to extremes. Character is a key requirement for adherence to a rational decision process. The ability to keep emotions from adversely impacting the investment decision process requires adherence to a policy. That adherence to a policy provides an enduring competitive advantage: the capacity to make rational (sane) decisions while other market participants behave irrationally. The capacity to think independently and objectively is also crucial; to keep your head while others are losing theirs. And finally, a clear understanding of self is fundamental in being able to know the limits of your "circle of competence"[2] and to stay within those limits.

Remember, you are not right or wrong because others say so. Being right or wrong is a function of your thinking being right or wrong. This book is a means to help you make rational investment decisions based on correct thinking rather than emotion. That is achievable through the use of process.

Why You Could Benefit from What I Have to Say

After fifteen years in finance and public accounting, I spent the next twenty-five years managing investment accounts on a discretionary basis for hundreds of clients through a wide variety of markets and economic conditions. Those twenty-five years of managing other people's money were concluded without experiencing a client complaint. Not a single one.

The reason for the absence of complaints was not because of an absence of "interesting times." Rather, it is believed to be because of two reasons:

First, each of the accounts was separately managed using a proprietary process utilized to replace emotion in the formulation of investment decisions.

---

2   A mental model conceived by and repeated referenced by Buffett and Munger that defines the boundary limitations of one's individual abilities.

Second, the details of that process were communicated to each client with transparency as to purpose, method, and results to provide confidence in the principles and policies of how their assets were deployed.

One of my clients was my Business Policy professor during my MBA studies. He was quite pleased with his initial results when he tried out the process for the first time. He had given me $200,000 to manage with the instructions to "show me what you can do." Six months later, his original investment was returned along with a profit that was several multiples of the original investment.

It was not at all a typical result, but the stars had aligned properly for him at the time. The professor's advice to me was: **"Don't ever tell anyone how you pick stocks!"** My response was simple: "Dick, I tell everyone. They're not interested. They all think that they have a better way."

This book is my formal attempt to tell everyone the fundamental principles underlying how:

- I picked stocks then (and continue managing investments now), and
- how readers can adapt these principles to both enhance their probability of investment success and reduce risk at the same time.

What was true then, decades ago, remains true today.

What Is NOT Working in the Market

The majority of individuals in the financial advisory industry conduct their practices based on underlying assumptions, policies, practices, and processes, many of which simply do not stand up to rational analysis.

They believe they have a better way.

Yet the sad reality is that the majority of investment managers, investment advisors, and their clients underperform in the markets, over time resulting in massive and unnecessary destruction of capital. Just look at how many of the full-time fund managers underperform their benchmarks. A quick review of the results of this performance reality can be found by looking at the reports periodically produced by a consulting firm by the name of DALBAR Inc., which describes itself as the nation's leading financial services market research firm. Those reports are titled **Quantitative Analysis of Investor Behavior (QAIB) Reports**.

For instance, the March 31, 2022, report "contains alarming findings that paint a grim picture of how the Average Investor behaved and performed in 2021."[3] The study concluded that the average investor earned more than ten full percentage points less than the market. They call this the "performance gap."

History shows that the gap between what the market provides in **investment return**, and what the average investor realizes as their **investor return** generally represents an underperformance of between 4–6% annually year over year.

The late John Bogle, the founder of Vanguard, documented that investor/investment underperformance gap in his own proprietary Vanguard funds was as much as 17% annually for the five years he studied. This was entirely attributed to investors' irrational behavior of buying what had gone up and selling what had gone down.[4]

The key to success is the opposite: Buying low and selling high. But history repeatedly demonstrates that human behavior, driven by the investor's own emotions, is the primary suspect in this mass misfortune.

---

3   This was the 28th year for the report. For more information, see: https://www. dalbar.com/Portals/dalbar/Cache/News/PressReleases/QAIB_PR_2022.pdf

4   See: https://www.etf.com/sections/features/6012-bogle-investors-are-getting-killed-in-etfs.html

Later in this book, the impact of performance variances is addressed, but to summarize it here, over a forty-year **investment horizon**, a 3% differential in performance results in two-thirds of the potential **terminal capital value** being lost. That is just a 3% differential. Not DALBAR's 4–6% usual performance gap, nor the more than 10% level that investors suffered in 2021, and nowhere near Bogle's observations of as much as 17% underperformance. So, rather than adding value, all the effort, talent, and intellect of all those investment advisors and their clients, while usually well-intentioned, serves to destroy capital for their clients.

There are multiple causes for this, but the usual prime suspects are but three:

1. Over-diversification in the industry is rampant.
2. Asset allocation is misunderstood and inappropriately applied.
3. The general lack of an appropriate written investment policy that provides a sound fundamental framework for making investment decisions and that *keeps emotions from undermining the investment process.*

As a result, the advisory firms' compliance departments and their legal counsels are fully occupied.

The Purpose of This Book

My purpose in writing the book is multi-factored.

First, it is intended to provide my spouse with both guidance and confidence to know she can manage her affairs in my absence.

Second, it is to provide individual investors and investment professionals with an example of how an articulated investment policy serves as the framework for making investment decisions and, if properly designed, keeps emotions from corroding the investment process defined in that policy framework.

Finally, I attempt to reciprocate in some small measure the countless instances of kindness, generosity, and mentoring by others of which I was the beneficiary. My way of doing so is by sharing how this portfolio manager approached the issues of managing risk, capturing opportunity, and reinforcing strengths.

Basically, I will explain "how to pick stocks" within the framework of a trilogy of a:

1. Written Statement of Investment
   Objectives establishing goals.
2. Formal Financial Plan that sets the timing of those ends.
3. Formal Investment Policy Statement
   creates the path to travel.

This book's content is not a magic formula for investment success. There are no guarantees that what worked for my clients and continues for myself will work for the reader. In the managing of investments, like in the preparation of a meal, the outcomes of recipes are generally chef dependent. That is the case here as well.

What You Will Find in This Book

Part A: The Primary Issues explores variables that impact investment outcomes: emotion; predictions of the future; over-diversification; asset allocation; valuation of investments; and risk.

Part B: Philosophy addresses several fundamental conceptual issues, beginning with knowing yourself and knowing what you own and why you own it. Then we will explore the usual suspects involved in adverse outcomes—ego, greed, and debt; the importance of independent thinking; the five characteristics of a great investment; and how to acquire an unfair advantage.

Part C: Process—The Why, What, and How looks at the key building blocks that process is built upon and how process enhances the investor's key to success: Focus. These tools can provide an investor with the ability to control their investment relationship with their advisors and evaluate the quality of the advice they receive.

Part D: Practical Application of the Art covers six practical applications of the art of investment management: 1. Assessing Investment Quality; 2. Estimating Intrinsic Value; 3. The Concept of Margin of Safety; 4. Diversification—The Costs and the Benefits; 5. The Art of Saying No; and finally, 6. Trade Execution.

Part E: Simplified Investment Process Examples looks at the teachings of Benjamin Graham, Warren Buffett's mentor, and the tool that was a driving force behind the success of Berkshire Hathaway. That tool, "The Margin of Safety," is the differential between market value and intrinsic value and includes the "Graham Formula," which is a short form estimation method for the estimate of intrinsic value.

This section also includes a demonstration of the practical application of those concepts; how one might put those pieces into action through an investment model referred to as "The Deals of the Dow." This is not the actual process I used as a portfolio manager, but rather a simplified version of that process provided as a starting point for you to develop your own means of thinking correctly about investing.

Part F: Tactical Implementation of Investment Strategy provides you with an eight-part summary upon which to build an investment program tailored to your own personal circumstances.

In conclusion, I hope that reading this book will give you an opportunity to change your thinking about investing. It is this change in thinking that will enable you to build your own individual investment processes and success. With an appreciation of the dramatic impact that a few extra points of performance can make, as demonstrated in "The 3% Difference" (the examples of the S&P 500 and Fairfax Financial Holdings book value relative rates of compounding over time), you can use the information in this book to *build your own successful investment program*, starting from the ground up with the three building blocks (a Statement of Investment Objectives, a written Financial Plan, and an Investment Policy Statement) as the foundation for a personalized investment process tailored to your unique circumstances.

PART A

The Primary Issues

> *It ain't what you don't know that gets you into trouble.*
> *It's what you know for sure that just ain't so.*
>
> —Mark Twain

The primary issues that cause problems for investors and investment managers alike come down to the fact that many of the underlying principles that are widely accepted as gospel simply are not true.

The primary subjects found to be problematic are:

1. Emotion (rather than process) drives investment decisions.
2. Predicting the future is a counterproductive use of time and focus.
3. Over-diversification is for those who seek protection from ignorance. It removes the ability to outperform and results in a lack of focus.
4. Asset allocation is used as an often-misapplied conceptual tool. Allocation of assets (both human resources and capital) is what you seek in the talents of management. It is broadly misunderstood.
5. A valuation of investments without a margin of safety represents risk.
6. Managing probabilities and certainty of outcomes is best achieved through the use of wide "Margins of Safety."

PRIMARY ISSUE #1:
EMOTION

Modern Portfolio Theory (MPT) assumes that markets are efficient, all information is known, prices reflect underlying value, and investors act rationally. That set of assumptions simply is not supported by the reality of human and market behavior. I would suggest that humans are first and foremost emotional beings. They make decisions based primarily on their emotions and then use their capacity for reason to rationalize why they made those decisions.

The investor's emotions are the primary obstacle to investment success.

Fear and greed are the primary human emotions that drive market fluctuations. As social media has made communications instantaneous, so too has it made the potential for panic and crowd-driven irrationality to impact markets at never before levels of rapidity. For examples, consider the crowd-driven short squeeze of Game Stop or the social media-driven collapse of Silicon Valley Bank that drove markets into turmoil with runs on banks worldwide.

Be fearful when others are greedy and greedy when others are fearful.[5]
—Warren Buffett

The Mr. Market Parable

"Mr. Market" was an allegory created by investor Benjamin Graham. Its purpose was to illustrate the irrational and often self-destructive behavioral traits of stock market investors and the risks of being caught up in the emotion-driven behavior of the market. Mr. Market was first introduced in the 1949

---

5   Berkshire Hathaway Letter to Shareholders, 1986

book *The Intelligent Investor*. The following is how Mr. Graham outlined his observations in chapter 8, titled "The Investor and Market Fluctuations":

> Imagine that in some small business you own a share that cost you $1,000. One of your partners, named Mr. Market, is very obliging indeed. Every day he tells you what he thinks your interest is worth and offers either to buy you out or sell you an additional interest on that basis. Sometimes his idea of value appears plausible and justified by business developments and prospects as you know them. Often, on the other hand, Mr. Market lets his enthusiasm, or his fears run away with him, and the value he proposes seems to you a little short of silly.
>
> ...you will be wiser to form your own ideas of the value of your holdings, based on full reports from the company about its operations and financial position.[6]

Three Choices

Here are the three choices for every investor concerning market fluctuations:

1. Ignore the fluctuations in the market.
2. Take advantage of the fluctuations using them to your benefit to buy cheaply or sell dearly.
3. Get caught up in the emotions of the market. Danger lies this way.

The first option, for the defensive investor, would be to take comfort in the reality that market history provides. While there can be long stretches of time where markets can show negative returns, history shows that in longer periods of time, the general trend is upward.

---

6   *"The Intelligent Investor,"* Benjamin Graham, Fourth revised edition, Harper & Row, page 108.

The second option, for the enterprising investor, would be to view market fluctuations for what they are: opportunities. When prices rise, it is the opportunity to sell at a favorable price, and when markets decline and the shares are quoted by the market at sale prices, it is an opportunity to acquire value at a discount.

The third option leads to disaster. Buying high (what has gone up) and selling low (what has gone down) is the path to ruin. Unfortunately, the reality of the markets show that this is the tendency of human behavior when emotions (fear and greed) are allowed to drive the investment process.

PRIMARY ISSUE #2:
PREDICTING THE FUTURE

Prediction of what is to come is a business best left to fortune tellers.

In the *Harvard Business Review* (July–August 2007), Paul Saffo attempts to lay the groundwork for effective forecasting in "Six Rules for Effective Forecasting." Boiled down to the essentials, it becomes: "Forecast Early, Forecast Often."

The amount of time and effort devoted to forecasting what the markets will do in the future represents a colossal waste of time, effort, and money. Yet that is where many financial professionals, economists, news commentators, and investment analysts devote the majority of their time.

For a practical example, take a look at the website of Yardeni Research. Ed Yardeni is a brilliant economist and the author of *Predicting the Markets*. A protracted look at the assembled charts and chapter headings makes the following three arguments for me.

First, regarding predictive forecasts, John Kenneth Galbraith, a Canadian born economist, author, US ambassador, and Harvard professor said: "The only function of economic forecasting is to make astrology look respectable."

Second, as for all of the efforts of Wall Street participants to predict the future, Ben Graham had this to say: "…if I have noticed anything over these sixty years on Wall Street, it is that people do not succeed in forecasting what's going to happen to the stock market." He then succinctly summarized the secrets to success: "There are two requirements for success in Wall Street. One, you have to think correctly; and secondly, you have to think independently."

Third and finally, it is far better to accept the realities that the markets present and use those real and present conditions as the available universe of opportunities at that moment. No forecasts or fortune-telling is required. Be present in the moment, focus on what is, and let what will be, simply be.

Directing one's energy and intellect into crafting and executing the appropriate response to the market realities present to the investor in the here and now is key to impacting outcomes. Spending one's limited resources trying to be the predictor of what may or may not happen in the future is counterproductive and detracts from developing appropriate responses to actual events in the present. That response will maximize the impact on the outcome.

The simple formula for a directed focus is:

E+R=O.
Event plus Response equals Outcome.

So, as Buffett advises, patiently wait for the fat pitch[7] to be thrown over the plate. Unlike in baseball, in investing there are no strikes being called. You can wait for your ideal pitch before taking a swing.

Viktor Frankl in *Man's Search for Meaning* describes the psychology of overcoming adversity. Focus the mind on what you can control, being your response. Those exogenous events, you cannot control.

Peter Jensen, in *The Inside Edge: High Performance through Mental Fitness*, describes the coping skills of Natan Sharansky, a Soviet dissident imprisoned for nine years. Asked how he survived the deprivations and the beatings, Sharansky replied: "I did not live in their world. I created a world in my mind where I was free... Every person has unlimited resources of resistance. I had

---

7　Outstanding Investors Digest, September 1998, Berkshire AGM transcript.

to treat them (the guards) just like the weather." He looked at them as something over which he had no control.

In summary, you cannot control the guards, good or bad. Like the weather, warm or cold, wet, or dry, you cannot control the weather. What you can control is: how you respond, in terms of how you think. You cannot change what is, but you have unlimited options in how you think and then, frame your response.

In the world of financial management, adversity should be embraced. It is the ultimate incubator of opportunity. It is also the greatest teacher if one learns from mistakes (both those of your own making but preferable those of others). You can capitalize on adversity in real-time if you are focused in the present on the opportunity, and not focused on forecasting what might be.

Devoting one's limited resources to predicting future events (which only liars can repeatedly do successfully) is a very ineffective and unproductive investment. Effective productivity requires a deliberate focus of one's limited analytical capacity.

First, focus on what "actually is" rather than what "might be."

Second, focus on the effective execution of the appropriate response to the situation in order to impact the outcome desired.

PRIMARY ISSUE #3:
DIVERSIFICATION RISKS AND BENEFITS

Worldly wisdom teaches that it is better for reputation to fail conventionally than to succeed unconventionally.

—John Maynard Keynes, *The General Theory of Employment, Interest Rates, and Money*

Diversification is grossly misunderstood and most often inappropriately utilized. Properly utilized it can partially reduce non-systematic risk. While there are many forms of risk, Modern Portfolio Theory focuses on two types: systematic (what might otherwise be referred to as market risk) and non-systematic (or specific company risk).

Diversification used improperly, beyond the limits of its benefits (a concentrated portfolio of five to ten uncorrelated positions), reduces both performance and focus. It also increases the primary risk that your decisions are wrong. More decisions, more potential errors. Thus, diversification is widely used as protection for those who know not what they do; it is *protection from ignorance.*

The focus on process to replace emotion is the single biggest key that an investor has available to achieve investment success. Diversification, in excess, dilutes focus. Although each additional holding (beyond five to ten securities) slightly reduces the portfolio non-systematic volatility (and it does not reduce systematic volatility at all), it reduces the investor's focus on knowing the details of each individual investment. This in turn increases the risk that you will do something wrong.

The biggest risk in investing is not knowing what you are doing; excess diversification beyond a few securities significantly increases that risk.

So why do almost all managed investment portfolios hold forty or more investments when more than 85% of the benefits of diversification can be achieved with a portfolio of only five uncorrelated securities? The answer is found in the words of John Maynard Keynes addressing the subject of reputational risk:

Finally, it is the long-term investor, he who most promotes the public interest, who will in practice come in for most criticism, wherever investment funds are managed by committees or boards or banks. For it is the essence of his behavior that he should be eccentric, unconventional, and rash in the eyes of average opinion. If he is successful, that will only confirm the general belief in his rashness; and if in the short run he is unsuccessful, which is very likely, he will not receive much mercy. *Worldly wisdom teaches that it is better for reputation to fail conventionally than to succeed unconventionally.*"

William F. Sharpe shared the Nobel Prize in Economic Sciences with Harry Markowitz and Merton Miller for their work on the Modern Portfolio Theory (MPT), the Capital Asset Pricing Model (CAPM), and measuring risk and return (the Shape Ratio). In studying the subjects in my MBA, Sharpe's book cited below had a quote that has always stayed with me.

A typical portfolio with equal dollar amounts of five securities will have 14% more risk than the most highly diversified portfolio imaginable… with ten securities will have 7% more risk, twenty securities will have only 3% more than the minimum.

—Noble Prize Laureate William F. Sharpe[8]

His message was clear: **"A little diversification goes a long way."**

But that is not how the industry came to adopt the use of diversification. In fact, the truly exceptional investors recognize his lesson and create exceptional returns with concentrated

---

8   William F. Sharpe, *Portfolio Theory and Capital Markets* (McGraw-Hill, 1970), p. 150

portfolios. The broad industry, however (remember 90% of investment results underperform), employ diversification to excess, and as a result, fail to add value.

See Appendix B for the mathematics underlying Sharpe's concepts of diversification. You will see that it shows that after the portfolio has eight to twelve uncorrelated issues, there is little if any benefit of further diversification but a significant cost in terms of the dilution of focus.

So, what is the alternative to diversification, especially in excess? The answer is focus. A focused or concentrated portfolio of only a few holdings provides the benefits of risk reduction, as Sharpe modeled, but retains the ability to add value in comparison to the overall market.

An anecdote in Alice Schroeder's *The Snowball: Warren Buffett and the Business of Life* illuminates the power of not being distracted.

"When Bill Gates first met Warren Buffett, their host at dinner, Gates' mother, asked everyone around the table to identify what they believed was the single most important factor in their success in life. Gates and Buffett both gave the same one-word answer: **'Focus'**."

When one looks at the portfolios of these two investors, it is clear they practice what they preach. Buffett is reported to have nearly all his net worth invested in Berkshire Hathaway. Berkshire, in turn, has an investment portfolio that has (as of the 2021 year-end) more than 70% invested in just four holdings.

William Gates has diversified his investments from Microsoft. However, his reported net worth of $134 billion at the time of writing is invested primarily in Berkshire Hathaway (45%); Waste Management (12%); Caterpillar (8%); CN Rail (7%); and Walmart, Ecolab, and Microsoft (4% each)—for a total of 82% in only seven holdings.

Prem Watsa, founder and CEO of Fairfax Financial Holdings, has 99% of his net worth in the shares of Fairfax Financial Holdings. Fairfax in turn had a common stock investment portfolio of $12.8 billion on December 31, 2022, where the seven largest investments represent 45% of the total.

> *Diversification is protection against ignorance.*
> *It makes little sense if you know what you are doing.*
> —Warren Buffett

22

PRIMARY ISSUE #4:
ASSET ALLOCATION

You're rarely all right or all wrong. So, divide your assets into two parts. Invest the first part divided between equities and bonds. Invest the second part depending upon the relative merits of the asset classes so that your maximum allocations range between 25% and 75%, depending on your objective to be defensive or opportunistic.

—Benjamin Graham (paraphrased)

Asset allocation is a significantly manipulated, misquoted, and misunderstood concept. The aim is to balance risk and reward. It does not replace the role of individual investment due diligence.

Frequent abuse of the concept includes a standard misquoting of Brinson et al.[9] which goes like this: "Asset allocation is the most important determinant of returns, accounting for more than 90% of performance." However, the truth of asset allocation, as represented, simply is not so. The Brinson study in question involved large, overly diversified pension fund portfolios that held $400 million or more in assets. Those portfolios are positioned through over-diversification so that they have no significant statistical difference from the markets in which they are invested because *their portfolios are so diverse that they are the markets.*

You cannot beat the market if you are the market.

The authors never intended for readers to conclude that stock picking had no impact.

A partial summary of the relative merits of the asset allocation study so frequently misinterpreted and paraphrased can be

9   Determinants of Portfolio Performance, Brinson, Singer & Beebower, *Financial Analysts Journal*, 1986.

found in a CFA Institute blog entitled "Setting the Record Straight on Asset Allocation."[10]

> Asset allocation relies on the notion that different asset classes offer returns that are not perfectly correlated and diversifying portfolios across asset classes will help to optimize risk-adjusted returns. The topic went largely unexplored until 1986, when Gary P. Brinson, CFA, Randolph Hood, and Gilbert L. Beebower (known collectively as BHB) sought to explain the effects of asset allocation policy on pension plan returns. In their seminal paper, "Determinants of Portfolio Performance," published in the *Financial Analysts Journal,* BHB asserted that asset allocation is the primary determinant of a portfolio's return **variability,** with security selection and market timing (together, active management) playing minor roles. BHB's 1986 study examined the quarterly returns of ninety-one large US pension funds over the 1974 to 1983 period, comparing the returns to those of a hypothetical fund holding the same average asset allocation in indexed investments. A linear time-series regression yielded an average R-squared[11] of 93.6%, leading BHB to conclude that asset allocation explained 93.6% of the **variation** in a portfolio's quarterly returns (not in the returns themselves).

In 1991, Brinson, Hood, and Singer published an update[12] to the BHB study. This examined returns from the 1977 to 1987 period and found a return variance of 91.5%, essentially confirming the results of the original study. In today's parlance, the BHB

---

10   See: https://blogs.cfainstitute.org/investor/2012/02/16/setting-the-record-straight-on-asset-allocation/

11   R Squared is defined as the coefficient of determination representing a measure about the quality of the fit to a model. It is a statistical measure of how well the regression line approximates the actual data.

12   Determinants of Portfolio Performance II, Brinson, Singer & Beebower, *Financial Analysts Journal*, 1991.

study went viral and almost immediately was incorporated into the marketing pitches of investment advisors.

But it did not go unchallenged. In 1997, William Jahnke published a critique of the BHB study[13], in which he argued: "The fundamental problem with BHB's analysis is its focus on explaining return **volatility** rather than portfolio returns. Investors should be more concerned with the range of likely outcomes over their investment planning horizon than the volatility of returns." Jahnke went on to warn: "**As the investor's circumstances or market opportunities change, so also should the investor's asset allocation.**"

Jahnke referred to the financial industry's exploitation and misrepresentation of the BHB study. He saw its embrace of the BHB study as an abdication of its active management responsibilities. Hood later pointed out: "Nothing in the original paper suggests that active asset management is not an important activity. It was not the point of our paper, and our goal was not to demonstrate otherwise.[14]"

In 2010, Roger G. Ibbotson in "The Importance of Asset Allocation," [15] noted an unpublished 1998 study by Jennifer and John Nuttall that found "forty-nine of fifty surveyed citations of the BHB study to be inaccurate."

So how can you effectively apply asset allocation as a policy? Once you have a clear written Statement of Investment Objectives (more on this later) and an understanding of your risk and return parameters, allocate your assets within a set range that can achieve the target return over time (this is your Financial Plan), while undertaking the minimum amount of volatility in those returns.

---

13   The Asset Allocation Hoax, William W. Jahnke, *Journal of Financial Planning*, February 1997.

14   Supra.

15   Financial Analysts Journal, August 2009

Next, design that allocation range to accommodate your investment process to allow you to adjust the allocations as market conditions change. This will lead to your Investment Policy Statement (IPS), which will be covered in more detail later in the book.

Ben Graham had a relatively simple approach to asset allocation. His first step was for an investor to define themselves as either **"defensive"** (a lender generally predisposed to having secure investment securities, i.e. bonds) or **"enterprising"** (seeking a higher return than that available in fixed income and willing to take risk and fluctuations in the pursuit of that goal).

For enterprising investors, he suggested dividing the available capital into two parts. The first half would be divided equally between equities and bonds. The second half would be deployed to whichever side of the asset allocation divide that appeared to have the most appealing attributes on a relative basis.

As a result, an enterprising investor's portfolio allocations would fluctuate somewhere between the minimum/maximum allocation ranges of 25% to 75% of bonds or stocks depending upon market conditions (think Mr. Market) as those conditions presented you with either: (a) opportunities to capture (by buying dollars for dimes in times of temporary adversity or widespread pessimism); or (b) risks to eliminate (by stepping back from markets where the excessive enthusiasm of participants was demonstrating that they were behaving in a cavalier manner about risk).

PRIMARY ISSUE #5:
VALUATION OF INVESTMENTS

Valuation is often based upon a particular metric that is relevant to the individual security: price to earnings, cash flow, sales, or book value. Alternatively, valuation may be based on comparisons to peers using multiple other metrics: market capitalization, enterprise value, EBITDA multiples, private vs. public market value. Simply put, there are multiple means of arriving at a valuation.

One with some merit is based on an analysis (in terms of **value line, regression analysis**) of the past trading history and then generally projected into the future (some forecasting required). The periodic diversion from the mean as represented in the value line charts is a useful indication of periods of over and undervaluation.

If one examines the annual high and low valuation of many of the securities covered in the universe of the value line reporting service, it is common to see a 30% to 50% annual variation from the annual high to the annual low in the market price quotation. This is consistent with the standard deviation metrics found by William F. Sharpe.

But this raises a most fundamental question: **margin of safety**. The margin of safety is the difference between the market value and intrinsic value. In my experience, a discount in market value from the estimate of intrinsic value of 1/3, or 33%, provides a minimum "margin of safety" for the protecting of capital. To see a major investment firm use the term **"intrinsic value"** in their research reports is very rare, which makes the Graham Formula very useful as a means of making your own estimates.

The term "intrinsic value" is an estimate of the present value of the future cash flows: the expected *future earnings stream* to be produced by an investment, discounted into a *present value* by the application of an appropriate discount rate adjusted for interest-rate levels and risk factors.

The wide swings in quoted market valuation of share prices are a frequent occurrence. But such fluctuations are rare in terms of changes in intrinsic valuation. As a result, those variations between market and intrinsic values periodically create opportunities that can be utilized to the investor's advantage both to enhance return and reduce risk. This is explored in more detail later by the example of practical applications titled the "Deals of the Dow." ©

Within the general market, individual securities have wide variations each year that are driven by public perception, emotion, headlines, and behavioral psychology (see *Extraordinary Popular Delusions and the Madness of Crowds* by Charles MacKay). These can be broad-based swings in markets in general (systemic) or focused on the relative assessment of the prospective outlook for an individual security (specific).

The investment industry couches the term "risk" within the catchphrase **"volatility."** Volatility is a two-sided coin. Side #1 represents a risk for those who do know not what they are doing. Side #2 represents opportunity for the investor with a prepared mind.

The margin of safety is a key concept of investing and can be used to manage risk by preparing the mind to think in the appropriate manner. For those who do not know what they are doing, volatility is the problem, and diversification is the solution. For those whose prepared mind has given them the ability to derive a conservative estimate of an investment's intrinsic value, fluctuations in market values represent opportunities.

On one side, investment opportunities are presented to the intelligent investor "on sale" representing the opportunity to acquire assets at discounts to intrinsic value. On the other side is the opportunity to exchange those same assets at prices that no longer offer a wide margin of safety, allowing the investor the ability to exchange them for assets that have greater investment appeal. In that context, volatility is the investor's friend, more akin to opportunity than to risk.

The chance to acquire shares at wide discounts to what they are worth provides a wide margin of safety. That margin of safety not only reduces risk, it also enhances returns—and not just in small measures.

PRIMARY ISSUE #6:
MANAGING RISK

In the old legend, the wise men finally boiled down the history of mortal affairs into the single phrase: "This too will pass." Confronted with a like challenge to distill the secret of sound investment into three words, we venture the motto: MARGIN OF SAFETY.

— Benjamin Graham in *The Intelligent Investor*

Investment risk is the failure to achieve your investment objectives, which as Graham defined them are but two: assurance of principle and an adequate return.

The **Management of Risk** requires four primary capabilities that provide the assurance of principle and enhance the adequacy of the return.

First, you must be able **to estimate an investment's intrinsic value** with a reasonable degree of confidence. Some individuals do this using the discounted cash-flow method, but this can also be done in a simplified method as provided in this book using Graham's Formula. Long before estimating intrinsic value became a service available through the Internet, Ben Graham provided a simple formula, known as the Graham Formula (see Appendix C), as a means of making that valuation estimation relatively quickly.

Second is the relatively simple **ability to assess the differential between intrinsic value and market value**. That differential in values, or discount, forms the basis of the "margin of safety." Fundamentally, this involves basic mathematics. An example of its application is provided in what is referred to as "The Deals of the Dow" (see Appendix D).

To make that margin of safety assessment is one thing. To have the courage to act upon that assessment while the crowd of public market participants behaves irrationally is something altogether different. To maintain the courage of your convictions and keep your head while all about you, others are losing theirs is not easy.

Third, you need the **capacity for analysis** to understand and assess the reasons for that differential in values; whether it is due to a *temporary issue* that will resolve itself in time or due to a *permanent impairment* of the economics of the business that will remain. That differential, when at a market level that represents a significant and temporary discount from intrinsic value, provides both a margin of safety for the "assurance of capital" and the opportunity for the enhanced probability of realizing "adequate returns."

Fourth is **the capacity to identify a catalyst** that can restore the market perception (a repricing) of the valuation of the enterprise. That might be due to internal or external factors. That assessment of the prospects for the business and economics of the underlying enterprise requires a higher order of independent thinking, analysis, and understanding. This is what Howard Marks of Oaktree Capital refers to as "second-level thinking."

Once you have formulated that assessment of intrinsic value and the margin of safety, gained an understanding of the causes of the discount, and identified a catalyst for change, two additional characteristics are needed: You need both **the courage to act on the conviction** and **a temperament that provides you with patience** as an investor.

It requires time for the markets to eventually recognize the intrinsic value of the investment. Regression to the mean is a powerful force in financial markets but can take time. As Charles McKay stated in his book *Extraordinary Popular Delusions and the Madness of Crowds*, "Men it has been well said, think in herds; it will be seen that they go mad in herds, while they only recover their senses slowly, and one by one."

If a picture would be worth a thousand words, try this picture: *Star Trek's* Mr. Spock, as the rational investor in control of his emotions ("logic would dictate..."), next to Homer Simpson, who is an example of the irrational side of human nature in the role of the manic-depressive "Mr. Market."

That is the role of the investment process: to formulate investment decisions within an appropriate framework and then *"to keep emotion from corroding that framework."* Expanding upon these subjects will be the focus of what follows.

PART B

Philosophy

*There are more things in Heaven and Earth, Horatio,
than are dreamt of in your philosophy."*
—Shakespeare

The knowledge that I or anyone can bring to the undertaking of making investment decisions has limits. However, the lessons that I learned along my journey are the foundations that shaped my philosophy. They are offered here so you might benefit with ease from that which I have learned, sometimes with difficulty.

- Know yourself, know what you own, and know why you own it.

- The usual suspects of ego, greed, and debt reappear with every cycle.

- Being the "house" brings certain advantages.

- Following what "they" say is often unproductive. Think independently.

- The "unfair advantage" is having a process and patience.

- Process protects the investor from emotions.

- Insight and wisdom come with continual learning.

FIRST AND FOREMOST, KNOW YOURSELF

> My years in Wall Street and business, in fact, became
> one long course in human nature... *how to balance the nature of*
> *things in this world in which we live with the nature of mankind.*
>
> —Bernard Baruch

There's an expression regarding the game of poker that applies to many zero-sum games. It goes like this: "If you've been in the game for twenty minutes, and you don't know who the patsy is, it's you."

Like poker, trading in the stock market is a zero-sum game. Every trade has both a winner and a loser. But trading is not investing. As Ben Graham once noted: "An investment operation is one which, upon thorough analysis, promises safety of principal and an adequate return. Operations not meeting these requirements are speculative."

The primary rule of the investment advisor is "know your client." The problem is that very few clients know themselves. A lack of self-knowledge is a primary obstacle to achieving investment success. In his book *The Intelligent Investor*, Ben Graham reminds us that the biggest obstacle to investment success is often the investor themselves, specifically the investor's own emotions. It's rare for individuals to be objective in measuring their investment performance. To do so would necessarily require an articulated investment policy and an appropriately defined benchmark against which to make performance comparisons. Without that benchmark, it's nearly impossible to make an objective assessment of one's role as an investor, so the same mistakes keep being repeated.

The results of self-directed investments are generally abysmal. This type of misdirected activity is a monumental destroyer of capital, opportunity, and in many cases, hopes, dreams, and lives. The statistical results for the self-directed investor destroy capital at a rate of 6% annually.

Wall Street is littered with the failed careers of people who, overall, were well prepared to achieve investment success. They had the right sort of education and plenty of experience, intelligence, and contacts. They were prepared in every way except for one thing: *temperament.*

Statistical analysis indicates that between 80% and 90% of investment professionals do not add value to the process. They consistently underperform their benchmarks over time. And that is the track record of the professionals. For individual investors, the reality is significantly worse. Authoritative figures such as John Bogle, founder of Vanguard, and the firm DALBAR have the studies to show the dismal results.

But it does not need to be that way! Adding value is achievable using a process to replace emotion in the making of invest-ment decisions.

Only one in ten people can be in the top 10%. If you believe you're one of the lucky ones, examine yourself against an objective measure. If you think you might be a member of the less fortunate majority, don't try to make investments yourself. Seek professional help. Your legacy depends upon it.

KNOW WHAT YOU OWN

I can admit it freely now. All my life I have been a patsy.
—Robert Cialdini[16]

In the normal world of supply and demand, price and demand are inversely related. As the price of something rises, the demand falls. As the price falls, demand increases. But that principle of basic economics is inverted in the stock market. There, the interest in owning a security increases as the price rises, and it decreases as the price falls. In Cialdini's book, *Influence,* he points out that this quirk in human behavior can be explained by the fact that people tend to substitute shortcuts for knowledge, so they often see *expensive* as the equivalent of *good.*

It's a common trait of human nature to assume that the primary symbol of investment merit is a rising market price. The reality, however, indicates that investment merit declines with each price rise. This is the primary conflict between human behavior and rational investment decisions. You ought to be able to explain the underlying merits of any investment you make (what you own, and why you own it) in terms that anyone could easily understand. It need not be complicated. A reasonable explanation should include the following key points: the sustainable competitive advantage of the investment in terms of the nature of the franchise, the strength of the balance sheet, the total returns on capital, the quality of earnings, and the way your interests as an investor line up with the interests of the company's management (i.e., how they make their returns).

Remember: There are two primary measures of an investment's value: first comes quality, then price. Quality is a judgment call. Price, on the other hand, is more straightforward. Price

---

16   Cialdini, Robert B., *Influence—The Psychology of Persuasion* (New York: Morrow, 1993), p. xi.

is what you pay. The higher the price paid, the smaller the investment's merit.

Value is the ultimate measure of an investment's merit: it represents what you get in quality per unit of the price paid.

KNOW WHY YOU OWN IT

If we had no liquid capital markets that enabled savers to diversify their risks if investors were limited to owning just one stock...

the great innovative enterprises that define our age—companies like Microsoft, Merck, DuPont, Alcoa, Boeing, and McDonald's—might never have come into being. The ability to manage risk, and with it the appetite to take risks and make forward-looking choices, are the key elements of the energy that drives the economic system forward.

—Peter L. Bernstein[17]

You should be able to explain how each of your investments fits into your articulated investment policy in terms of objectives (the "why you own it"). Of course, this presumes that you have made the effort to develop a program that will be the underlying foundation of your investments. This program must operate in good and bad markets and in changing economic conditions. Without a guiding policy, it quickly becomes easy to lose one's way in the investment process.

As a first step, it's a prerequisite that the investment is under-priced. Important issues include why the investment is cheap; why the undervalued pricing is temporary (and represents an opportunity); what the real estimate of value is and how large the resulting margin of safety is' and what will cause the market to recognize the true value of the stock.

Warren Buffett once said that it would greatly benefit the investment decision process if, upon graduation, each student was provided with a punch card that had twenty holes, one of which was punched each time an investment decision was made.

If the graduates only got to make twenty decisions during the course of their careers, they would put a lot more thought into

17   Bernstein, Peter L. *Against the Gods: The Remarkable Story of Risk*, New York, Wiley, 1998, p. 3

each one. Years later he also said that *the majority of the wealth created at Berkshire Hathaway was the result of only eight decisions over thirty-five years.*

One frequently hears it said that a certain investment is undervalued. Just as often that opinion is based not on the facts discovered in objective analysis, but rather on a hunch or emotion. Therein lies the danger. If you can objectively calculate the approximate value of an investment's intrinsic worth, then you'll see that the pricing of the market will sometimes offer the investment to you at a significant discount. In that discount lies the margin of safety. That margin of safety protects capital. It usually serves as the ultimate validation for the acquisition of an investment.

Investing involves a great number of uncertainties that are best dealt with by managing the probabilities. Peter Bernstein deals with the subject brilliantly in *Against the Gods*.[18] "The odds—the probability of winning—are all you need to know for betting in a game of chance, but you need far more information to predict who will win and who will lose when the outcome depends on skill as well as luck. There are card players and racetrack bettors who are genuine professionals, but no one makes a successful profession out of shooting craps. Many observers consider the stock market the result of skill combined with luck, or is it just the result of a lucky gamble? Bernstein returns to this question in chapter 12."[19]

In short, if you buy on bad news and sell on good, you will practice the widely known, but little-followed, primary rule of investment success: "Buy Cheap and Sell Dear."

---

18   Bernstein, Peter L. *Against the Gods: The Remarkable Story of Risk* (New York: Wiley, 1998), p. 3.

19   ibid, p. 14 [Chapter 12, "The Measure of Our Ignorance," p. 197] See also Chapter 15, "The Strange Case of the Anonymous Stockbroker

THE USUAL SUSPECTS:
EGO, GREED, AND DEBT

It is easier to resist at the beginning than at the end.
—Leonardo Da Vinci

Toward the end of the movie *Casablanca*, when the general is shot, the prefect of police orders his staff to round up the usual suspects. Likewise, toward the end of every business cycle, a good many investments and their investors get shot—financially. The cause of their collective demise can generally be attributed to the usual suspects: ego, greed, and debt.

This is especially true in the real estate and financial sectors.

In 2007, Bank of America CEO Ken Lewis remarked that: "We were close to a time when we would look back and realize that we did some very stupid things." For those who have lived through enough cycles to be personally familiar with the usual suspects, that comment turned out to be prophetic.

Pride is the greatest human sin. Some call it ego, but whatever you choose to call it, individuals are led to believe that because they've been successful, they must therefore have a special ability to become even more successful.

A modest amount of success can lead to an entourage of flatterers, and soon we start to believe our own press. Once ego begins to dictate the decisions, expectations grow, and greed appears in the form of "if some is good, then more must be better." Debt, the enabler of getting to more, faster, arrives on the scene. The benefits of leverage can only serve to advance the process exponentially.

In today's world of finance, the game is increasingly stacked toward "heads we win" and "tails you lose." The best defense against this uneven distribution of risk is the subject of the next chapter.

Heraclitus once said that "nothing endures but change," but I would offer this amendment: "Nothing endures but change *and human nature.*"

BEING THE HOUSE

Does the company have a management of unquestionable integrity?

> *The management of a company is always far closer*
> *to the assets of the company than its shareholders.*
> *The number of ways...those in control can benefit...*
> *at the expense of the stockholders are almost infinite."*

—Philip A. Fisher[20]

One way to avoid the perils of human nature would be to understand the inherent incentives that exist in any relationship. It's easy to see that the cards are stacked against you when the management of the investment has no skin in the game. If you are the one who takes the risk, and they are the ones who get the reward, then the motivation is to increase the risk without limit.

Read Roger Lowenstein's *When Genius Failed: The Rise and Fall of Long-Term Capital Management* to get a deeper understanding of this phenomenon.

As the returns increase, the lion's share of the rewards are the management's, and when the game fails, the loss is yours. Heads "they" win, tails you lose. That's how it works in far too many modern investment management relationships, whether they are publicly traded companies, hedge funds, or commission-based (especially discount) brokerage accounts.

This type of relationship could be characterized as a promoter-based sales relationship, where management makes money *from you* rather than *with you*. **It's much better to align your interests with those of the investment's management.**

---

20   Fisher, Philip A., *Common Stocks, Uncommon Profits* (New York: Wiley, 1996), p. 50. Taken from Chapter 3, "What to Buy—Fifteen Points to Look For." The fifteenth and most important point is: *management integrity and stewardship.* "The average investor is not a specialist in the field of investment. He usually gives but a tiny fraction of the time or mental effort to handling his investments that he devotes to his work... misconceptions, and just plain bunk that the general public has gradually accumulated about successful investing." (Ibid., p. 51)

In the "good old days," an ideal partnership could be found where one partner contributed the capital, another the toil, and they shared the proceeds. Both shared a vested interest since they both had a significant investment at risk, be it capital or labor.

In this traditional relationship of shared proprietary interest, both parties have a vested interest in the risks and the rewards. In such cases, management makes money *with you*, as opposed to *from you*. If management has more skin in the game than you, then if they steal from you (or try to delude you), they are stealing from themselves (or deluding themselves).

Now you own a piece of the house, and the game is fairer. There's still risk, but the undertaking is one of shared risks and common interests, rather than opposing interests. Now, instead of a zero-sum game (where one wins and the other loses), both parties participate in the creation of value.

Understanding the underlying incentives in the business relationship *is key to having mutually beneficial investment relationships.* Only then can one avoid being the patsy in a zero-sum game.

"THEY SAY"

Don't follow the crowd—
there are fads in the market just as in women's clothes.
The ability to see through majority opinions…
can bring rich rewards."
—Philip A. Fisher[21]

Something that everyone knows isn't worth knowing.
—Bernard Baruch

Nothing is more ubiquitous and counterproductive in the financial world than the client who responds to investment advice by uttering these words: "Yes, but *they* say…"

Usually, the "they" in question refers to the media pundits on television investment news channels. The information they offer is just that—information. While some useful information can be gleaned occasionally from TV news programs, it's not guaranteed to be accurate, nor are these reporters prescient. Wisdom and insight are seldom bandied about in the public forum. In recent times, the pundits' motives can be quite nefarious.

It is impossible to gain a competitive advantage from the information disseminated through mass media. Quite the reverse. News can be manufactured and transmitted to manipulate security prices. It would serve investors well to remember the purpose of mass media. In the words of a successful newspaperman: "The purpose of news is to fill the white spaces between the advertisements." In the movie based on the novel *The Shipping News,* actor Gordon Pinsent tells a potential newspaper employee how to write an arresting headline: "Terrible Storm Threatens Tiny Fishing Village." The alert candidate asks, "But

---

21   Philip A. Fisher, *Common Stocks, Uncommon Profits* (Hoboken NJ: John Wiley, 1996), p. 129.

what if there *is* no storm?" To which Pinsent responds, "Tiny Fishing Village Spared Terrible Storm."

There is all too often no direct relationship between news and truth, nor in news is there any altruistic interest in the readers' welfare.

Consider for a moment the controversy represented by the defamation action of Dominion Voting Systems vs. Fox News. Settled for US$787.5 million, the evidence that came to light in the emails of the parties involved demonstrated the sad reality of journalistic integrity.

I wish Walter Cronkite, a paragon of journalistic integrity, were still here. As he would say, "And that's the way it is."

The overriding purpose of mass media is to sell advertising. The more controversial the commentary, the better the ratings, and the better the ratings, the higher the revenues. Nowhere in what "they say" is there an alignment of interests in your welfare.

On the contrary. The idea is to sell something in a zero-sum game whose purpose is to separate you from your money. Occasionally it can be a blatant stock manipulation, and the media is merely a tool. Increasingly, in this world of Internet influencers, the spread of ignorance by the uninformed is too much with us, often motivated by ulterior motives.

Think of the term "Fake News" and the motivation of the speaker.

There is a hierarchy of information. First, it's just that—information. The world is filled with an excess of information that is more appropriately labelled noise. Then there is useful information. Useful information is acquired through diligence. With experience, useful information can become insight. Occasionally, with insight, judgment, and experience, information becomes real knowledge, and then potentially knowledge leads to wisdom.

The book titled *The Richest Man Who Ever Lived* by Steven Scott is a guide to the *Wisdom of Solomon* as delivered through the thirty-one Proverbs. It has an interesting assessment of the subject of wisdom and how it relates to the creation of wealth. If knowledge is power, wisdom is wealth. Those who have access to knowledge, insight, and wisdom do not squander it by sharing it with others who are not prepared to value it (or think that they can obtain it for nothing).

There is no free lunch.

Broadcasting or publishing certain opinions will often give the words credibility that they are not necessarily entitled to possess. When it comes to mass (or especially social) media, it is safer not to believe anything you read or hear, and only half of what you see. Although with the development of artificial intelligence, even that last half is increasingly in doubt.

THE UNFAIR ADVANTAGE

All I ever wanted in life was an unfair advantage.

—W.C. Fields

If there is a single best friend of the investor, it is time. But to make use of it, you must have enough patience to wait for the right opportunity. Warren Buffett calls this the "fat pitch."[22] You also get to define the size of the strike zone, and the smaller you make it, the better off you will be.

Everybody has a circle of competence: an area in which they have a unique ability. The trick is to know the boundaries of that circle and stay within them. Professionals (doctors, lawyers, and yes, even accountants) will often assume that their expertise in one field gives them special skills in another. It is an expensive conceit. But hubris is not limited to professionals.

To approach the market with humility, knowing only that you do not know, (knowing the boundaries of your abilities and staying within them) is the best defense. However, you must also have the courage of your convictions, or you will never be able to act on the opportunity.

So, the keys are:

- Know the limits of your abilities.
- Have the discipline to stay within them.
- Have the patience to wait for the opportunity to come to you.

What else makes a successful investor? Six qualities are important: humility, courage, discipline, patience, commitment to a rational fundamental decision process, and the ability to learn from mistakes. (Learning from your own mistakes is a must,

---

22 O.I.D., Supra

but the cost of tuition is much cheaper when you learn from the mistakes of others.)

The Importance of Process Driving Performance

If one were forced to reduce the many elements of successful investing into a single element, it would have to be PROCESS.

Incorporated into both a prudent and carefully applied process, all the other pieces come together in harmony. The center of that process should be focused on two factors: investment quality and the margin of safety; always in that order.

In the **commissioned-based investment advisory business**, the focus is on generating sales rather than the investment decision process. The revenue (commission or a quota, like the discounters and professional associations' captive firms) is generated from transactions rather than performance, so patience is anathema. To someone who comes into the office and must find a method of generating revenue through trading (remember the zero-sum game), patience is not a productive component of a successful business model.

If you have commission-based accounts, you are motivating your advisor through incentives to generate transactions. Behavior follows incentive. Like Pavlov, expect them to behave according to what you give them as a reward. The more trades, the more revenue. That is the primary conflict between advisor and investor.

Front-end commissions are the investment equivalent of a hit-and-run. Those not confident in their ability to perform, or lacking any intention of being held accountable, find it better to get paid in advance.

Find someone capable whom you know, like, and trust. Hire that person on an asset-based retainer. That way, they prosper as you prosper. They only get paid as they perform, so your interests and those of your advisor are aligned toward the same result.

In the **fee-based investment management business**, the focus is on performance, and successful performance is a function of the process. Revenue is a function of the assets under management. The process drives performance, in the creation of value for the client, which in turn is what attracts the assets.

THE VALUE OF PROCESS

Ignorance speaks, knowledge listens.
—Jimi Hendrix

Process is the investment equivalent of pulling all the pieces together.

The required tools and attributes are combined into a repeatable standard of prudent practice. See the Foundation for Fiduciary Studies' *Prudent Investment Practices that have been adopted by most levels of government in the USA.* [23]

This prudent process begins in one place—with the development of a written Investment Policy Statement (IPS) that articulates the objectives, risk tolerances, investment philosophy, investment process, and asset-allocation parameters for the assets to be invested. Without a written IPS, there is no real protection from the strong emotional forces of news, events, individuals, and uncertainty.

In my practice, I have yet to meet a single investor who can articulate the components of successful investing without going through the process of developing a written IPS.

Instead, one often sees emotionally driven decisions that are made one day and reversed the next. Of course, for commission-based investment advisors, that is not necessarily a bad thing, as one usually generates more revenue from emotionally driven trading where a client is whipsawed between greed and fear. Perhaps that is why most individual investors are not encouraged to invest the time to develop an IPS designed around a process.

---

23   https://www.sec.gov/comments/4-606/4606-2340.pdf and https://www.fi360.com/resources/prudent-practices/ and https://www.aicpa-cima.com/search/prudent+investment+practices although these are firewalled sites requiring registration.

DALBAR is a financial-services market-research firm. The DALBAR investor behavior research studies repeatedly show that the average, individual investor underperformed the markets by 4% to 6% annually. The primary culprit was emotional trading: buying what had gone up (buying high) and selling what went down (selling low). According to John Bogle,[24] the late founder of Vanguard, that loss of return (*investor* returns vs. *investment* returns) approaches as much as 17% annually for individuals using Bogle's own Vanguard exchange-traded funds (ETFs).

One never sees an advertisement for an investment that boasts, "Our price went down 50% last year, sale, sale, sale." But in hard fact, buying when things are on sale does work, both in the supermarket and in the stock market—especially when buying quality (on sale) that is priced below what it is worth.

The only way I know to make that happen (buying quality when it is on sale) is to substitute a *disciplined, articulated process* for the manic-depressive swings of human *emotion*. If there's one thing that will provide an unfair advantage, that W.C. Fields always sought, it is PROCESS.

The road to success is taken by those with the patience to develop and focus on a prudent investment process.

---

24   Bogle: Investors "Getting Killed" in ETFs, https://seekingalpha.com/article/144052-bogle-investors-getting-killed-in-etfs

ADVICE, INSIGHT, AND WISDOM

Darwin's lesson is that even people who aren't geniuses can out-
think the rest of mankind if they develop certain thinking habits.

—Peter Bevelin[25]

There is no shortage of advice in this world, particularly when people are paid to provide it. But some individuals are better advisors than others. How can one tell the difference? Look to the source.

Is the source a person of proven accomplishment in terms of performance? Are you certain? How does one verify what one thinks one knows? What lessons are to be learned from observing the Bernard Madoff[26] fraud tragedy, for example?

Newsletters are not a dime a dozen, but they should be. They are published by people who know how to write. They are published by people who can and do sell their words. That is their talent and their business: selling advice. With the explosive growth of the Internet, the industry of "social media influencers" fills the inboxes of modern technological devices with noise that at best is worthless and often hazardous.

Newsletters and social media posts almost certainly are *not* published, however, by people who can perform through the effective application of investment wisdom. The possession of that rare talent is priceless, and it's not given away for a monthly subscription to a newsletter or in a YouTube video that is a functional advertising tool for the capture of eyeballs.

There are various ways to gain access to worthwhile insights. Warren Buffett is one example. The annual Chairman's Messages

---

25   Peter Bevelin, *Seeking Wisdom: from Darwin to Munger*. Post Scriptum AB, 2007. PCA Publishing LLC.

26   For a detailed examination of Madoff, see the article from *Town and Country* magazine: https://www.townandcountrymag.com/society/money-and-power/a9656715/bernie-madoff-ponzi-scheme-scandal-story-and-aftermath/

he writes for the Berkshire annual report provide excellent insights. Many people share their knowledge and insight and have proven their track records. They are often very willing to share, but they're not selling their wisdom and insight as commodities.

Look for "the hook" to tell the difference. Ask yourself what it is that they are really selling.

When I was asked in my role as a portfolio manager to prepare investment guidelines for the next generation of a successful business family's members, I began the process by reading every "Letter to Shareholders" that Warren Buffett wrote as CEO of Berkshire Hathaway. Each pearl of wisdom was catalogued and amalgamated into categories.

Those were then enhanced with the teachings of his mentor, Ben Graham from *The Intelligent Investor* and *Security Analysis*, along with principles outlined by Phillip Fisher in *Common Stocks and Uncommon Profits*, and the teaching of Keynes in *The General Theory of Employment, Interest, and Money*. I then combined these with insights contained in *The Outstanding Investor Digest* (no longer in print), along with many perceptive observations from successful investors and my personal experience of having worked for (and learned from) an extraordinary collection of entrepreneurial leaders, to prepare the investment guidelines requested by this client.

Three Observations

That leads us to three important observations.

1. The process of reading and learning from others is far more efficient than learning from your own mistakes. For readers who have an interest in learning from some of the great investment minds that I find exceptional, please make use of the provided bibliography of outstanding investment readings in Appendix G.

2. Successful investing is a process of continual self-education; one either moves forward, ripening one's understanding, or one stagnates and goes to rot. Ripen or Rot—it is a personal choice.

3. You can improve with age. The physical limitations and the realities of old age may humble, challenge, and disappoint, but the ability to gain additional understanding is limitless.

PART C

Process—The Why, What, and How

*An investor's own emotions are the biggest obstacle
to investment success.*

Why: Process is the means of overcoming emotion in investing decisions.

What: Defined objectives/formal policies lead to independent thinking.

How: Personalized parameters to constrain decisions within boundaries.

The Result: A Plan/A Path/Defined Objectives/Focus/Confidence

The Prerequisite Building Blocks:

> The Statement of Investment Objectives
>
> The Financial Plan
>
> The Investment Policy Statement

PROCESS: THE WHY

To invest successfully over a lifetime does not require a
stratospheric IQ, unusual business insights, or inside information.
What's needed is a sound intellectual framework
for making investment decisions, and the ability
to keep emotions from corroding that framework.

—Warren Buffett

The right framework for your investment strategy must consider your unique circumstances and objectives. Articulating the framework in a written Investment Policy Statement (IPS) strengthens the emotional discipline required in rising markets to avoid buying at the top and in adverse markets to prevent selling at the bottom. It is important to remember that market prices are driven by supply and demand. This means the general consensus is usually on the wrong side of the trade because when a majority has the same "popular" opinion, it quickly impacts market prices. As the majority trade their positions, the minority on the other side of the trade can sell at a high price or buy at a lower price.

Hence, you may prosper by "giving the people what they want." When everyone else is buying, you sell. The price will have been bid up. When everyone is selling, a modest bid will suffice to buy at the then depressed prices.

With a clearly articulated written Investment Policy Statement (IPS) and a well-defined investment process, an investor can patiently wait for opportunities to knock. Then, with defined parameters in place, you can choose only those opportunities that suit your unique circumstances.

Warren Buffett's quote at the beginning of this section, which was also the preface to Ben Graham's *The Intelligent Investor*, is worth repeating as it is the key to investing success: "To invest successfully over a lifetime does not require a stratospheric IQ, unusual business insights, or inside information. What's needed is a sound intellectual framework for making investment decisions, and the ability to keep emotions from corroding that framework."

The process provides both the "sound intellectual framework" and "the ability to keep emotions from corroding that framework" if the investor has the temperament to stick within the limits of the process. The process allows the wise investor to remove the major obstacle to investment success: their own emotions.

The process makes results repeatable. The process provides you, as a thoughtful investor, with the ability to constantly improve your choices by incorporating enhancements of things that worked, thereby building upon each success.

Adverse markets should be embraced, for they contain the seeds of opportunity. Investors equipped with a formal process are prepared to (in the words of Rahm Emanuel, former White House chief of staff), "Never let a crisis go to waste."

Process is the key to having a prepared mind that is equipped and ready to turn adversity into opportunity.

PROCESS: THE WHAT

> Regimentation and repetition make skill sets become
> second nature,
> so in the face of adversity one can maintain control
> of the functional skills *that make it possible to prevail*
> *when others are seized by fear and panic.*
> —*Unknown*

> *If you can keep your head*
> *when all about you are losing theirs...*
> —Rudyard Kipling, from "If"

Your investment process should be centered on an Investment Policy Statement (IPS) that embodies investment guidelines that fit your unique objectives as an investor. A constructive way to define objectives is as a way of demonstrating value. Three effective methods to create value are through: eliminating fear (reducing risk); capturing opportunity (realizing specific goals); and enhancing existing strengths. If you define investment policy guidelines incorporating these concepts of value creation, the policy will, by definition, encompass your primary objectives.

These points of value creation address powerful investor emotions: fear, greed, and ego. With the risks and opportunities known, the destructive influence of the market's crowd psychology is reduced. Ownership of shares from seasoned, large capitalization issuers with above-average dividend yields might be one such objective. If a relatively new issue comes along without a long record of earnings, dividends, and clear financial statements, it's easy to exclude it from the portfolio because it does not match the objectives of the policy. When everyone else is enthused, the policy maintains emotional discipline.

The subject of ego is successfully confronted when the strengths that need to be reinforced are addressed. If you quantify a capital sum, identify a fixed time horizon, and establish a rate of return for achieving specific goals, then it's easier for you to dismiss peer pressure, media commentary, and sales pitches. Recognizing your strengths and weaknesses is part of knowing yourself. Finding and articulating the means to enhance those strengths makes you stronger with each step.

To form a solid investment process, start with a clear statement of objectives and a list of risks to eliminate, opportunities to capture, and strengths to reinforce. Having an articulated investment process allows you to make good decisions faster (being first) and make them better (better is step one in becoming best). Having a uniquely tailored process will make you different. Few investors have an IPS or the ability to articulate an investment policy, so the path of least resistance is to follow the consensus of the crowds.

PROCESS: THE HOW
The Investment Policy Statement

Cycles in markets are inevitable, irrepressible, and indispensable. Even if some all-knowing central bank could create a state of economic perfection—measuring out growth in ideal, non-inflationary doses, neither too much nor too little—human beings would respond by paying too much for stocks and bonds. In this way, they would restore imperfection.

—James Grant[27]

There are over 25,000 money managers in North America, and each one claims a unique process.

There are a seemingly an unlimited number of investment products, with new ones being created daily. There are individual stocks and bonds—but which ones? Exchange Traded Funds—but which exchanges and which issuers? And should you go with leveraged or unleveraged, long or inverse, hedged or unhedged? Mutual funds or separately managed accounts (SMAs)? Hedge funds? While there is no right answer for all investors, there is a right answer for each investor. Each one must find their own path.

What follows is one—my process that I developed as a portfolio manager.

That process managed to add value for over twenty-five years, relative to the performance of the underlying market benchmarks, by an average excess return (Alpha) of over 3% annually.

For me as a portfolio manager, it comes down to a list of "musts." Here is a personal list of items that this process must incorporate into the objectives. As an investor, you might

27   "The Trouble with Prosperity", James Grant (of Grant's Interest Rate Observer), 1996, New York, Crown Publishing.

consider a separate list that aligns with your priorities to start building your Investment Policy Statement (IPS).

INVESTMENT POLICY STATEMENT "MUST HAVE" DEFINING CHARACTERISTICS:

- It must be simple. Less is more in most things—math as well.

- It must be focused, by limiting diversification to a few issuers (twenty maximum).

- It must be diversified between industry sectors (35% sector maximum limit).

- It must be low maintenance in operation (four quarterly cycles).

- It must be repeatable (clearly defined process).

- It must emphasize capital preservation over return (wide margins of safety).

- It must add value in terms of performance against its markets (Alpha).

- It must be adaptable (flexible asset allocation range limits).

- It must be prudent and demonstrate due diligence (research and analysis).

- It must incorporate the lessons of the masters (history and lessons of others).

The outcome of any recipe with identical ingredients is always chef dependent. No two practitioners will arrive at identical results or conclusions. Of the varied approaches to investment management, the above list is but one of many. What makes it unique involves circumstances and nuances beyond the scope of this manual. However, this policy has value creation at its center, and the core of value creation has three parts:

1. Eliminating risk
2. Capturing opportunity
3. Reinforcing strengths

WHAT PROCESS ACHIEVES

In the real world of investing, the vast majority of investors (>90%) realize results that underperform the general market investment returns by wide margins. According to numerous research reports, the margin of underperformance is both wide (more than 4% annually), and persistent over long periods (measured in multiple decades). In absolute dollar terms, the amount of capital destruction that this results in is simply enormous.

To put the numbers in broad perspective, the New York Stock Exchange (NYSE), which is the world's largest market capitalization of publicly traded securities, represented a market capitalization of $30 trillion in 2018. The typical returns on those invested equities average approximately 10% annually ($3 trillion). The annual underperformance of 4% means collective annual investor losses on the order of $120 billion.

The simple fact is that this unfortunate state of affairs need not be this way. The primary cause is not the commissions and fees of advisors (although they do contribute to the issues of performance). It is the reality of human nature that investment decisions are made based on emotion rather than with a disciplined framework for investment decisions based on a rational process that prevents emotions from undermining the framework.

In the typical commission-driven "sales agency" advisor/client relationship, emotion is a tool that drives sales. Think fear and greed.

In a fiduciary advisor/client relationship, there is the potential for improving the fundamental terms of the relationship.

The fiduciary role involves a higher standard of care on the part of the investment advisor. Along with that higher standard of care comes a higher level of liability. It is insufficient to appear to be diligent. A fiduciary must be able to demonstrate their exercise of prudence and due diligence.

One purpose of this book is to provide you, as an investor, with the means of assessing the investment advisor relationship through basic due diligence to evaluate the fundamental framework for the investment decision process.

Through this process of due diligence, you will be able to know that you are getting the right advice and taking the appropriate actions to address any issues. You will then be able to go forward confidently to achieve your goals and objectives with the benefit of competent counsel and constructive advice.

The fundamentals of the due diligence process are built upon "Standards of Practice" codified into various statutes. For the purposes here, the Uniform Prudent Investor Act (UPIA) contains the fundamentals that can be simplified around three building blocks that every investor can use to guide their assessments of both the advice they receive and the investment management decisions that are made in the deployment of their assets:

1. A Statement of Investment Objectives (*The Purpose*)
2. A written Financial Plan (*The Plan* for getting from here to there)
3. An articulated Investment Policy Statement (*The Path* traveled)

Most investors have told me that they have them in practice, but fewer than one in ten can produce them when asked. Even then, when the investor can produce the formal documentation, often the actual deployment of their assets is in contradiction to the stated constraints that the documents specified.

The reality is that the institutional imperatives of the advisor or asset manager's business model will often overcome the written directives of the individual investor over time. That is why ongoing due diligence is necessary to ensure that the investor's priorities remain paramount.

In short, the investment process must have *a purpose to achieve, a plan for action,* **and** *a path to follow.*

As time passes, actual results can be objectively assessed against heroic intentions. This permits learning, adjusting, refining, and improving to adapt to the realities of changing circumstances.

Perhaps most important is the ability to have an anchor to keep emotion from corroding the "sound intellectual framework" for making investment decisions that are articulated in the investment process as part of the IPS.

The single largest obstacle to investment success is the investor's own emotions. People make decisions with emotion and then use reason to rationalize those actions.

Process, properly utilized, replaces emotion in the making of those decisions. It becomes the "regimentation and repetition" of skill sets that, when actual results are measured against planned intentions, allows for continual learning, adaptation, and improvement.

FOCUS

"An important advance is that emotion now looms much larger in our understanding of intuitive judgement and choices than it did in the past."
—Daniel Kahneman, *Thinking Fast and Slow*

The enhanced ability to focus is a prime benefit of a written Investment Policy Statement (IPS).

We are bombarded daily by massive amounts of inputs from television, radio, and the Internet. These inputs are designed to elicit behavioral responses in service to the interests of the speaker, not the listeners.

Our perceptions are often lacking in effectiveness. We tend to perceive what we are looking to find. The "reticular activating system" or RAS is part of human psychology that focuses perception on what is being sought, often blinding the individual to what else is there.

In *Thinking Fast and Slow,* Daniel Kahneman reviews how intense focus on a task can render a person effectively blind, even to stimuli that would normally attract attention. Another interesting book on this topic is *The Invisible Gorilla: How Our Intuitions Deceive Us* by Christopher Chabris and Daniel Simons.

We can be blind to the obvious and blind to our blindness.

Emotion can be the blindness "that corrodes the investing decision framework." Removing emotion from the making of investment decisions is possible through the use of policy and process enabling the investor to "navigate the noise" of extraneous inputs.

This repetitive nature of the process makes it possible to maintain focused attention, freeing you to effortlessly focus on the resources at hand and ignore the inputs that are designed to induce emotions of fear (flight or fight) or greed (blinding one to the intellectual decision framework). With repetition, the investment process can enhance concentration on the task at hand (focus). Not having to exert self-control to deal with emotional what-ifs, allows you, as an investor, to enter into a state of "flow" or concentrated focus on the issues of investment policy and process. This results in superior investment decisions and, in turn, improved investment results because of a superior, focused thinking process.

Charles Darwin is remembered for his concept of evolution. Among the concepts attributed to Darwin are "survival of the fittest" and "adapt or perish." In the introduction to *Seeking Wisdom,* Peter Bevelin refers to Darwin's special talents, which were identified by Charles Munger in one of his lectures on "Worldly Wisdom." The quote attributed to Munger goes like this: "Darwin's lesson is that even people who aren't geniuses can out-think the rest of mankind if they develop certain thinking habits."

Bevelin then directs the reader to the annual reports of Berkshire Hathaway (Buffett) and Wesco Financial (Munger) as the best educational tools for how to think about investing and business. He concludes by saying, "If I had listened to them earlier in my life—so many expensive mistakes would have been avoided."

CONSERVATIVE CONVICTIONS AND COURAGEOUS EXECUTION

Investing can be compared to several sports analogies.

Charles Ellis in *Winning the Loser's Game* does just that in terms of tennis. In that game, the object is to return the ball over the net in a manner that makes it difficult for the opponent to do the same. The winner is the player who makes the fewest mistakes, thus allowing the opponent to defeat themselves with their own mistakes.

In golf, mistakes cost strokes. Keeping the ball in play is paramount. The fewer the mistakes, the lower the score. In golf, the rule is to plan a conservative strategy (center of the fairway), then execute it with confidence (aggressive swing). The successful player has a practiced routine (process) that is repeated, thus enabling concentration on the task (focus on the ball) with deliberate control of focused attention.

In investing, the policy is your set of the rules of the game (designed for your objectives and plan), and the process is the deliberate attention to eliminating the emotions so often involved with monetary decisions.

Warren Buffett would say everyone has a circle of competence that they need to define. "It matters not, how large the circle is." What matters is "knowing where the boundaries are and staying within them."

Of course, this is simple to say and difficult to do.

Consider golf. Fairways and greens are the limits, stay within them, and the score will take care of itself.

Define your process in the form of a written investment policy statement, keep it simple, adhere to it, and the results will follow. Ultimately, this leads to a simplified example of the Graham Formula (which follows later in Appendix C), and the margin of safety, the keystone of my investment process as a portfolio manager. But first, let's examine the three building blocks that are prerequisites in the development of the investment process.

THE STATEMENT OF INVESTMENT OBJECTIVES

In 1996, Donald Trone (et al.) published *The Management of Investment Decisions*, seeking to provide investment professionals with "a practical manual that lays out the step-by-step process for the proper management of investment decisions." That book followed the 1994 publication of *Prudent Investment Practices* in conjunction with the American Institute of Certified Public Accountants.

Being a CPA is how I encountered Mr. Trone and the Foundation for Fiduciary Studies and came to focus on the investment process in my discretionary investment management practice.

In the above publications, the "Statement of Objectives" is the beginning section of the standard template for the Investment Policy Statement (IPS).

In my practice, it became apparent that the most important part of serving clients was to arrive at a clear and mutual understanding of the objectives as the first step in creating value.

This simple task of articulating the objectives for the client (often in conflict with the objectives of the advisor) is of paramount importance. It is both the "ready" and "aim" portions before proceeding to the "fire!" portion of executing the client investment journey. Without that being completed appropriately, the process can result in "ready, fire, aim," which is usually problematic.

A major tool in defining the objectives appropriately came to me courtesy of Dan Sullivan's work at The Strategic Coach Inc. Among his many tools and talents is something called the DOS questionnaire (Dangers, Opportunities and Strengths). Akin somewhat to the SWOT analysis (Strengths, Weaknesses, Opportunities, Threats), DOS focuses on creating value for others by eliminating Dangers, capturing Opportunities, and the enhancement of existing Strengths.

In turn, this is a fundamental part of The Strategic Coach mantra of the entrepreneurial process of creating value.[28] This process has three parts:

1. **Leadership** to provide a sense of direction.
2. **Relationship** to provide a sense of confidence.
3. **Creativity** to deliver the benefit of solutions that would otherwise have been omitted.

So here is how the DOS tool from The Strategic Coach can be used by any individual to help them create value for themselves by exercising their own sense of leadership, relationship, and creativity with or without the participation of an investment advisor.

It begins with evaluating the present situation and defining the objectives. The first question goes like this: "If we were sitting here three years in the future looking back upon today, what would have to have been achieved to feel happy about the progress?"

Dan Sullivan calls that question the "R factor" question (where R refers to Relationship), and it is a clear defining indicator for the potential of client relationships. But outside of advisor/ client relationships, the "R" factor question is something we should each ask ourselves to examine our personal objectives.

That single "R" question has two very asymmetrical responses from people. The first, usual response to the question is long, involved, and detailed, providing factors for consideration that are very personal to the individual's present situation and the hopes and dreams for the future.

---

28   Dan Sullivan, *The Great Value Creator Escape, 2001* and *Time Breakthrough: The Strategic Coach*, Toronto, Ontario. These publications provide more detail on the creation of value.

Second, for the individual who can respond positively to the question in terms of identifying goals and ambitions, three additional questions follow:

1. What three dangers do you feel need to be eliminated or mitigated to best enhance your confidence?
2. What three opportunities do you most want to be able to capture?
3. What three existing strengths do you feel you have that are most important to build on and enhance?

Simple yes. But extraordinarily powerful.

With your response to those dangers, opportunities, and strengths (DOS) questions, you now can develop a written statement of objectives that creates meaningful value for yourself on a unique and highly personalized level.

I believe that every individual should take the time to go through that DOS process, and from that process be able to develop a formal statement of investment objectives for their personal situation. For the purposes here, it relates to investing, but the process can apply to a far larger range of issues for other purposes as well. This exercise allows an individual to articulate a clearly defined sense or vision of direction that can be used to define their objectives, establish purpose, and build confidence.

In addition, the DOS process provides the opportunity to demonstrate creativity by delivering solutions to eliminate or at least mitigate any fear and uncertainty associated with the articulated dangers. It also increases the probability of capturing the identified opportunities and being able to articulate the existing strengths, build upon them, and potentially take them to an entirely new level.

Earning a fixed rate of return, targeting the addition of a small measure of excess return or Alpha over market benchmarks (maybe), and reducing risk through diversification or asset allocation is the usual set of industry standard goals set in investment objectives. *However, they have limited importance and are woefully lacking in creating real value for clients.*

That is why the early steps to develop a written Statement of Investment Objectives are so important. It is essential to invest the effort to examine in detail your (or a client's) current situation, and then create a framework to articulate real priorities and motivations. Then you will really "know yourself," and this is the first and foremost step in developing a statement of investment objectives, then a financial plan, and finally an investment policy to bring it into reality.

Purpose, plan, and path are the three components required here.

If you have a defined purpose (statement of investment objectives), a plan (written financial plan), and a path to travel (the investment policy statement), you then have the basic blocks to build upon. Once you have these tools, you can use them to provide direction to your investment advisor to follow and be evaluated against for performance.

Having those three components (Purpose, Plan and Path) in hand puts you in control of the investment relationship.

THE FINANCIAL PLAN

The development of a financial plan begins with an inventory of the present situation; what you have in assets minus liabilities equals equity.

Once the present situation is assessed, then quantification of the items in the Statement of Objectives can be performed, and SMART goals can be selected. "SMART goals" are goals that are: Specific, Measurable, Achievable, Realistic, and Time specified.

The development of a formal, written financial plan can be quite expensive and time-consuming. It is usually best left to a professional who is skilled in the process. There is an entire field of titled Professional Financial Planners, but the specific credential granting of this title is less than well-controlled. Often the offer of a financial plan is merely a hook so that a financial planner can gain access or insight into the assets available to invest. Most professional accounting firms will offer the service for a fee, and most investment advisors include the service as part of their offering for no additional charge over the associated costs of asset management.

Use caution and be aware of both the level of professionalism and potential conflicts of interest when engaging the services of a financial planner. There are many different credentials.

In my experience, getting a properly produced, detailed Financial Plan is a major source of benefits to an investor. These benefits include:

- Raising the level of professional care.
- Reducing both the risk faced by the investor in their financial affairs as well as the level of psychological stress they were under (which they may not have realized they were experiencing until they had their printed results in hand).

- Enhancing their confidence to move forward in pursuit of their objectives.

- Quantifying expectations for progress (which will then be defined as objectives).

- Enabling regular evaluation of progress (and thereby the advisory relationship) by measuring actual results against heroic intentions.

THE INVESTMENT POLICY STATEMENT

The most important duty of the fiduciary or trustee is the development and ongoing maintenance of an Investment Policy Statement (IPS). A good, well-communicated IPS can go a long way in preventing disaster.

— D.B. Trone et al. in *The Management of Investment Decisions*

The IPS is usually a standard template designed by the investment management firm's compliance department because of its importance in the issue of fiduciary liability. The real value appears in times of adversity—whether it is to control the rising animal spirits in bull markets or steady the fears associated with bear markets. In either case, it is a means of controlling emotions that serve so often to deny the investor success.

Usually, there are six parts:

1. Purpose and Background (statutory and other)
2. Statement of Objectives (primary importance)
3. Guidelines (risk, asset classes, timelines, return targets)
4. Process for Investment and Manager Selection (critical)
5. Security Limitations and Constraints (boundary defining)
6. Controls, Duties, Responsibilities, Monitoring, and Reporting

You can choose from a variety of sources and formats, but it must be written, regularly reviewed and revised as circumstances evolve, and adhered to in the deployment of the investment capital.

Step outside the bounds of the terms of the IPS as a fiduciary, and any claim of prudent action is lost.

PART D

Practical Application of The Art

"Define your circle of competence.
It matters not how large the circle is.
What does matter is knowing where the boundaries are
and staying within them. "
—Warren E. Buffett

A man has to know his limitations.
— Clint Eastwood as Dirty Harry

The comments in this section bring together the philosophy discussed, and the policy laid out in the previous two sections to demonstrate how those principles come together in practice to produce investment results that add value beyond the underlying market returns. Adding value in terms of results consists of two parts that work concurrently:

1. Producing returns on investments that are above the underlying market benchmarks.
2. Incurring lower-than-market risk.

However, neither of these objectives has much relative importance unless the results achieve the absolute returns required in the investment objectives that are specified in the Financial Plan.

These comments reflect the actual approach I used in the management of a North American large capitalization equity portfolio for a diverse group of clients. It is but one example of many possible alternatives. It certainly worked for me and will suit my ever shrinking and increasingly focused individual circle of competence.

In this section I cover six practical arts:

1. Investment Quality
2. Estimating Intrinsic Value
3. The Concept of Margin of Safety
4. Diversification—The Costs and the Benefits
5. The Art of Saying No
6. Trade Execution

PRACTICAL ART #1:
INVESTMENT QUALITY

These five characteristics are not of my design. They summarize a collection of key points, many arrived at through summarizing key points made by Warren Buffett in his annual "Letters to Shareholders." The result of those and other readings, tempered by my own experience in corporate finance and investment management, came to the following five primary considerations of investment quality:

1. Market Dominant Position (king of their respective hill)
2. Balance Sheet Strength (little or no debt)
3. High Returns on Total Capital (ideally 15% or more)
4. Real Earnings (confirmed by cash flow
   net of capital expenditures)
5. Propriety Management (management
   that thinks like owners)

One of the strengths of the Value Line research reports is that they provide the basic information from which the reader may discern the measure of each of the above characteristics.

From a universe of securities with those characteristics, individual investments are selected when those candidates become available for investment at significant discounts to their intrinsic values.

When that happens, it is possible to build a portfolio of exceptional quality for significantly less than its real worth. What follows is a detailed summary of each of the five characteristics.

While there are other issues to consider in assessing an investment candidate, experience teaches that these categories cover the majority of issues. Restricting candidates to those meeting most or all five criteria focuses the investment universe for consideration to just the best candidates. Sometimes three out of five is acceptable, but the price must be right. Your investment outcome is determined when you buy correctly, not when you sell.

Quality is always #1.

Price is important in determining the margin of safety but secondary to the following five differential characteristics of quality.

Market Dominant Position

> *Competition Can Be Hazardous to Your Wealth.*
> —Warren Buffett

Warren Buffett would rather own the shares of a great business acquired at a reasonable price, than own the shares of a reasonable business acquired at a great price. So, what makes a great business?

The answer depends on context and one's view of the world. Many would see tobacco, arms, or chemical businesses in a different light than others. Ethical constraints are a relevant issue for all business franchises. The perception of the business is growing in importance, as are Environmental, Social, and Governance issues (ESG).

Does the business provide value to the customer? If it does a better job of providing value, then it eventually ends up dominating the field in which it operates and acquires monopoly-like qualities as it marginalizes the competition.

The main point here is that a business franchise doesn't achieve "king of the hill" status merely by accident. To achieve market dominance, a host of sustainable competitive advantages must be called upon. Once a business does come to dominate the market, it becomes a Herculean task for its competitive challengers to displace it. In military terms, it is the equivalent to the analogy of "holding the high ground." The dominant market position has sustainable competitive advantages on many layers. The number one characteristic of quality is a market-dominant franchise that represents unique, sustainable, competitive advantages.

A market-dominant franchise is a fundamental part of building a moat around the business that makes it difficult for competitors to mount a sustainable competitive challenge. For a detailed analysis of the subject, see *Blue Ocean Strategy: How to Create Uncontested Market Space and Make the Competition Irrelevant* by W. Chan Kim and Renée Mauborgne.

Balance Sheet Strength

> *Liquidity is like oxygen.*
> *When plentiful, no one thinks about it.*
> *When scarce, it becomes all you can think about.*
>
> —Warren Buffett

For the market position and other sustainable competitive advantages to be realized in the investment results, the second quality characteristic is that the firm must have staying power.

That is represented in the quality of the balance sheet, where little or no debt is the goal. Jamie Dimon, CEO of JP Morgan refers to this as a "fortress" balance sheet. When challenging economic times come, and they do arrive sporadically, strong companies have access to capital that weaker, more leveraged competitors are unable to access. When liquidity is scarce, they get to "eat the competition's lunch." The more levered competitors fall to the inevitable challenges of the vicissitudes of the business cycle. The rating of the company's credit can be a significant, sustainable, competitive advantage when time becomes a challenge. In graphic terms, Buffett describes it like this: "Liquidity is like oxygen. When there is lots of it available, no one thinks about it. When it becomes scarce, it becomes all you can think about."

That is why one should embrace adversity. In difficult times, the financially stronger enterprise can benefit from the misfortunes that are visited upon the weaker competitor and grow market share as competitors withdraw from the marketplace. No place is that more apparent than in the insurance underwriting cycle of what is called a "hard market" for the pricing of underwriting risk.

Adversity, in Buffett's terms, can also be revealing: "It is only when the tide goes out that you get to see who has been swimming naked."

When markets become difficult, and liquidity is scarce, the merits of balance-sheet strength become a sustainable competitive advantage. The strength of the balance sheet has a great differential impact on access to liquidity.

High Returns on Total Capital

Returns on capital can be a measure of both the quality of management and the financial productivity of a business. Some entities are so capital-intensive or so characterized by competitive pricing challenges that they can't earn significant returns on the capital that has been entrusted to their stewardship, regardless of managerial talent.

A business product might be commoditized by competition or become outdated due to technological change—or worse still, both may occur. Some businesses manage to escape being commoditized through the creation of brand strength, while others do so using proprietary processes, intellectual property, or competitive barriers to entry associated with scale.

Deceptively high returns on *equity capital* can be produced through the miracle of leverage and accounting legerdemain.

But high returns on *total capital,* without the magic of leverage, are key.

In compellingly attractive business enterprises, the returns on capital are so strong that, over time, the company can buy back their shares and you end up seeing a business that operates with little or no need for any shareholder equity on the balance sheet.

Real Earnings: Net Free Cash Flow
After Capital Expenditures

A characteristic of an excellent business is reported income that is "real."

The creative energy that goes into producing the annual report for a public company varies between issuers and accounting firms. As an accountant and a writer of many annual reports for public companies, I have learned that discretion can impact reported results. Likewise, once you have spent sufficient time reading annual reports (yes, some people, not many, actually do), you come to realize that there is a wide range in their credibility. Most range near accuracy; some say more by what they omit than what they reveal; and then some are pure fiction.

One sure way to eliminate fiction from the analysis of reported results is to measure the **reported earnings** against **net cash flow** (net cash flow after capital expenditures required to maintain the operating plant and equipment). Where the cash flow net of capital expenditures, or "CAPEX," exceeds reported income, the accounting is likely conservative. Where the reported income exceeds net cash flow, the company may be taking liberties in the accounting policies, or as some might say: "Burning the furniture to keep the lights on." One of the leading defensive utility stocks in Canada routinely ran a surplus in reported earnings ahead of net cash flow for years at a time, followed by repeated periodic restatements of earnings due to "non-recurring items" that wiped out the overstated reported earnings from the preceding years.

If you are promoting the shares for sale to the public (perhaps because management's stock options will be worth more upon exercise), your adaptation of accounting principles would be in sharp contrast to those used by an enterprise owned by a single shareholder who had the reporting of lower levels of income as a motivation to reduce the current cash expense of income taxes to be paid.

This leads to what is arguably the ultimate question: *the character of management,* which is explored further in the next section. Having capital at risk is a major differentiating factor in one's thought process. To check if management thinks like shareholders and has their interests aligned with yours, look to see how much of the company's shares are owned by management. If the officers and directors of the company own less than 1% of the shares outstanding, is it reasonable to think that their motivation and decisions are focused on the long-term prospects of the shareholders as owners of the business? Or might the focus instead be on the compensation consultants' report supporting the monumental increases in their annual bonuses and awards of stock options?

Those differences can have a significant impact on the accounting function and the discretionary recognition of reserves and accruals. For example, consider the question of expenditure. Often a case can be made that an expenditure was for an expense during the current reporting period or for the benefit of multiple years into the future. Depending on the treatment of this expense— whether it is charged to expense, impacting earnings, or capitalized to be amortized over future periods—it can have a significant impact on reported earnings but little impact on cash flow.

Imagine this: Upon arriving at the local hardware store, a customer asks the owner, "How's business?" The owner opens the cash register, looks in the cash drawer, examines the day's receipts, and looks back up, responding, "Pretty good today."

That is the measure and fundamental importance of net cash flow.

Proprietary Management[29]

The investment should possess characteristics of a franchise
and sustainable competitive advantages
that are so strong that any fool could run it,
because if you own it long enough, any fool will.

—Warren E. Buffett[30]

What is the mindset of management? *Do they think and act like owners or promoters?* Do they make their money as a long-term owner of the company *(along with you)* or, do they make their money as promoters of the company *(at your expense)?* Are they honest stewards? What are their incentives?

Far better is a company whose managers have substantial amounts of their capital at risk. That way, they share the same objectives as the shareholders because they are shareholders. They think like owners with a long-term orientation for the business decisions they make.

When management has no capital at risk or "no skin in the game," the focus is more short-term, such as getting more perks (putting nice new leather in the Gulfstream) or boosting the share price (so the options can be exercised at the maximum price). Then they move on to the next term posting on the career ladder. They may think in terms of "get mine and get gone."

Is management there for a long time or a good time?

---

29   *The Outsiders* by William N. Thorndike (Harvard Business Review Press, 2012) provides eight case studies of extraordinary leadership examples of shareholder-focused value creation.

30   Buffett, Warren, Chairman, Berkshire Hathaway. "Letter to the Shareholders"

Extraordinary talent in leadership is rare and valuable. The talent of leaders who create unusual value often center on allocation of resources. That asset allocation is two-part: allocation of financial resources and allocation of human resources.

The essence of any business enterprise is its people. Management that possesses a proprietary interest in the long-term success of the enterprise recognizes the importance of its human resources. In the present economy, there are more job openings than available workers, and there are always alternate opportunities available for the most productive of employees. Witness the unfolding issues at the change of management of Twitter in 2022 and contrast that to the management style of Mary Barra, CEO of General Motors.

One measure of the commitment to employees that can keep them engaged is the presence of a defined benefit pension. That pension is a rare benefit today and, in most cases, its assets only partly fund its obligations. However, when pension assets are in a position of surplus, overfunding the actuarial obligation, it indicates that the management takes their obligation to their employees seriously, and they are competent in investing capital.

Management lacking demonstrated talent in those key asset allocation characteristics undermines the investment merit of the organization.

> *Does the company have a management of unquestionable integrity?*
> *The number of ways…those in control can benefit…*
> *at the expense of the stockholders are almost infinite.*
>
> —Philip Fisher, *Common Stocks, Uncommon Profits*

> *If you do not trust the character of management, no degree of discount from intrinsic value and no quantity of collateral can be sufficient to warrant that capital be placed at risk.*
>
> —J.P. Morgan, from *The House of Morgan*

PRACTICAL ART #2:
ESTIMATING INTRINSIC VALUE

Many shall be restored that are now fallen,
and many shall fall that are now in honor.

—Horace in "Ars Poetica"

Underlying the theory of common stock valuation is the **capital-ization of future earnings**. But what should be used to estimate future earnings? What interest rate should be used to estimate the present value (capitalize) of the estimated future earnings stream that the investment is expected to produce?

The answer is found in the concept of **Equity Risk Premium.**

Investors can be segmented into two distinct groups based on what they favor. Generally, they are either *enterprising* inves-tors as "owners" of stocks willing to suffer the wide swings of quoted market values and the uncertainties of outcomes or *defensive* investors (think "lenders" and bonds where there is a covenant of repayment).

The differential returns achieved by the two investors' classes vary by cycle, but long-term returns fall roughly into estab-lished ranges.

There is an equity risk premium associated with returns of stocks for undertaking the uncertainty and risks of equity ownership (and forgoing the covenants of secured lending).

Over long periods, the stocks' returns average about 50% more than bonds, but the variation from period to period is highly uncertain. From 1925 to 1998, the average return to an investor from an AAA-rated ten-year corporate bond was about 5.9%.

Over the even longer long term (from 1810 to 2008), the average return on stocks in the US equity markets was about 8.5%. The equity risk premium rewarded to owners (8.5%) over lenders (5.9%) was 2.6% or approximately 50% more than the return of bonds.

Since rates of return vary with both time and cycles on a relative basis, one can use an equity risk premium of 50% as an approximate expectation of relative return for the *additional risks* associated with an investment in equities.

This becomes an important determinant in deciding what value to place on the estimated future earnings of an investment. It also establishes an expected discount rate to use when you are estimating intrinsic value.

One quick way to determine an investment's capitalized value can be found in *Security Analysis,* by Graham, Dodd, and Cottle.[31] It uses *forward earnings, the growth rate in earnings,* and the *market interest rates* to determine an appropriate estimate of the capitalized present value of future earnings. The method has come to be known as the "Graham Formula" (Appendix C) for valuing common stocks.

> Value = Current (Normal) Earnings X (8.5 + 2 X g),
> where g is the expected annual growth rate in earnings per share.

Analyst reports are produced for a variety of reasons, but rarely do they place an intrinsic value on a company. Instead, they attempt to estimate the unknowable bi-polar behavior of the market crowd based on the pricing of the shares in the future based on manic-depressive swings in mood and in reactions to exogenous events taken from the past as well as manic expectations for future results. (See *Extraordinary Popular Delusions and the Madness of Crowds,* by Charles MacKay, tracing the history of widely aberrant crowd behavior such as the Dutch tulip mania.)

---

31   Benjamin Graham and David Dodd. *Security Analysis* (New York: McGraw-Hill, 1951), p. 537–8.

The behaviors of crowds reacting to the reports of results that deviate from expectations (earnings surprises) results in wide swings in market valuations. As a result, there will always be swings in market pricing like the movement of a pendulum as investor sentiment swings between excess enthusiasm and pessimism.

For that reason, the intelligent investor should embrace adversity. It is by the response of the crowd of market participants to events that the market offers opportunities to acquire shares at significant discounts from intrinsic value. The same swing to enthusiasm will provide the investor with the opportunity to sell shares at prices that are near to, at, or more than underlying intrinsic values.

Interest-rate fluctuations will impact the valuation of equity capitalizations. Changes in earnings will also have an impact. It is important to keep in mind, however, that the widest variation comes not from those two economic factors but rather from the behavior of the participants in the market, driven by emotional reactions to news headlines and short-term events.

The level at which the market will price the shares, particularly in the short term, may often have little relationship to the intrinsic value of the reasonably estimated future earnings power of the business.

While general market valuations frequently fluctuate, and a standard deviation in prices can be 20% to 30% or more annually, both for individual securities and for the market in general, intrinsic value changes very little in comparison. The intrinsic value (the sum of future earnings discounted to present value today using an appropriate discount rate) of quality enterprises will generally change little over time due to short-term exogenous factors. But the market prices of that same enterprise's shares will swing widely from period to period.

As a result, evaluation of an opportunity expressed in the short-term variation of market prices, relative to intrinsic value (discounts or premiums), can provide the opportunity both for excess returns and for risk reduction.

One means of identifying those variations of market prices from intrinsic values is to focus on the concept and calculation of the margin of safety inherent in each investment candidate.

The Graham Formula provides a shortcut to an approximation of value as a starting point. Its use reduces the number of investment candidates under consideration to a much smaller universe upon which detailed analysis is warranted.

PRACTICAL ART #3:
THE CONCEPT OF MARGIN OF SAFETY

In the old legend, the wise men finally boiled down the history
of mortal affairs into the single phrase, "This too shall pass."
Confronted with a similar challenge to distill the secret of sound
investment into three words, we suggest the motto:
"MARGIN OF SAFETY."

—Benjamin Graham in *The Intelligent Investor*

Once you can estimate the worth of an earnings stream, then you can determine if the quoted market value reflects a significant discount (or premium) to intrinsic value. Even high-quality issues will be priced at a market valuation in any calendar year that swings widely from high to low.

Typically, that variation in market value ranges between an annual low that is 30% to 50% below the market-price annual high (or more). Events rarely impact the future cash flow of a company by anything approaching that level. Yet the market price of almost every one of the thirty issuers in the Dow Jones Industrial Average varies by that much every year. These fluctuations in price present opportunities for the investor, independent of the variations in the overall market. Even so, many academics and investment professionals continue to assume the market is efficient.

Investing has two parts: assurance of principal and an adequate return. "Margin of Safety" is key to both. Using a Buffett analogy, you could drive a truck that weighed 9,800 pounds over a bridge rated for 10,000 pounds, but why? If assurance of principal were the categorical imperative, then the margin of safety would dictate that the larger the discount in the price paid for the investment compared to the estimated intrinsic value (tonnage rating), the greater the assurance of principal.

The greater the margin of safety is, the greater the assurance of the principal. If you can buy a dollar (of intrinsic value) for fifty cents (of market value), then you have the luxury of being confident that if your estimate was off by 25%, you still have a wide margin of safety. You can still safely drive the truck over the bridge.

Smallish trucks, riding over big, strong bridges is ideal.

But here's the bonus: If your estimate was somewhere near correct, and the market eventually recognized that a dollar was a dollar, the probability of your achieving an adequate return has just increased, and not by a little. The margin of safety not only enhances the assurance of the principal, but it also enhances the adequacy of returns.

You can equate the process with a simple metaphor: "Buying dollars for dimes."

PRACTICAL ART #4:
DIVERSIFICATION: THE COSTS
AND THE BENEFITS

A typical portfolio with equal amounts in five securities
will have only 14% more risk (measured by standard
deviation) than the most highly diversified portfolio imaginable.
A typical portfolio…with ten securities will have 7% more risk than the
minimum possible; while twenty securities
will have only 3% more risk.[32]
—William F. Sharpe

Everything should be made as simple as possible, but not simpler.
—Albert Einstein

Since we can remove, or at least minimize "specific company risk," and this can be achieved with only a few securities, why do most managers choose to have forty or more holdings in a portfolio? Could it be because they are more concerned about the career risk of being shown to be wrong than by failing to add value?

John Maynard Keynes in *The General Theory* said: "It's better to fail conventionally than succeed unconventionally."

Buffett puts it as a question: "Why place your money in your fortieth favorite holding rather than your third?"

As a practicing portfolio manager, my preference was to have a total portfolio of ten securities divided between the US and Canadian markets. I was asked by management to amend the investment policies for the accounts of my discretionary managed clients to have between fifteen and twenty holdings.

---

32   Noble Prize laureate William F. Sharpe, *Portfolio Theory and Capital Markets*, McGraw-Hill, 1970, p. 150. See also Appendix B.

The resulting ability to add value over the underlying bench-marks suffered as a result. The performance was still adding value—just not as much.

The resulting "North American Equity" portfolio benefited from diversification of several kinds:

First, by asset class. Portfolio holdings were divided between Canada and the US. As a Canadian investor fishing for an opportunity, would you not want to fish in the best-stocked pond? The United States remains the largest, most dynamic, most innovative, and most investor-friendly market in the world.

Second, by individual securities. There was a maximum of ten holdings in each of the US and Canadian asset classes.

Third, the portfolio was diversified by sector. No sector can comprise more than 35% of the portfolio. With that sector diversification and the further constraint limitation that no one security represents more than 10% of the total portfolio, there were three levels of diversification. Three levels might be overdone, but it was more effective and done with far fewer individual holdings than the typical managed portfolio of forty to seventy positions in a single market.

The Benefits of Limited Diversification

By investing in only two markets, focus is not lost by looking everywhere at once. Further, risks of geopolitical issues, cur-rency risks, accounting risks, and systematic risks of other jurisdictions that lack long histories of private property rights supported by robust traditions of common law are eliminated.

By having no more than ten positions in total in each market, the focus was maintained using the concept of "span of control." Fewer than eight results in less-than-optimal effectiveness. More than twelve, and the effectiveness is compromised. Ten (actually eight to twelve) is the ideal span of control for effectiveness. It also optimizes the benefit of diversification by reducing specific (company) risk by 93% to only 7% of what it might otherwise have been using William Sharpe's Noble Prize-winning concepts contained in his 1970 *Portfolio Theory and Capital Markets.*

Now that I am retired, my portfolio is back to a maximum diversification of ten holdings. Focus is enhanced, performance is improved, and both effort and risk are significantly reduced.

"Risk lies in not knowing what you are doing."[33]

If you limit diversification, you increase your focus. That increase in focus is how you can reduce the risk of venturing outside of your circle of competence.

Restricting investment efforts to high-quality businesses will simplify the process and increase the probability of success. Looking at fewer companies will help you to understand them in greater detail. Eliminations can be made quickly if there is not a wide discount to intrinsic value. Little time is required to make the above evaluation on a regular cycle. Once you get to the best ten (ordered in priority of quality and then the margin of safety), STOP!

The investment world then gets less complicated, the focus becomes more precise, and the resulting probability of investment success increases.

The difference between stupidity and genius
is that genius has limits.
—Albert Einstein

---

33   "Risk comes from not knowing what you are doing." Attributed to Warren Buffett speaking to Columbia University Business School graduate students in 1993 by reporter Jim Rasmussen who wrote about the event in the January 1994 "Omaha World-Herald".

PRACTICAL ART #5:
THE ART OF SAYING NO

People think focus means saying yes to the thing you've got to focus on.
But that's not what it means at all. It means saying no to the hundred
other good ideas that there are. You have to pick carefully.

—Steve Jobs

This part of the "Practical Arts" section might well have been a continuation of the subject of diversification. But "saying no" is so important that it deserves its own heading.

If "focus" is the key to success, as Buffett and Gates say it is, it is also the antithesis of diversification. With so many opportunities and so little time, saying no is an essential tool.

Saying "no" is fundamental, but it also has factors that can become refined to the point of making saying "no" a highly developed art.

When my spouse and I moved into our house more than twenty-five years ago, the former owner had left a handwritten note taped to a hidden pull-out work platform that extended from his built-in office desk titled "How to Say No Without Offending":

1. Listen—Understand
2. Say "No"
3. Give My Reasons
4. Offer Alternatives to Demonstrate Good Faith

That note remains in its original place more than three decades after it was written by my friend and mentor, Norman Newman. Norman was very successful in his businesses, extraordinarily generous in his helpful contributions to many individuals, and a strong supporter of his community.

He was a busy man but managed to find time for the things that he felt were priorities. To do that and to have the time he generously devoted to others, he had that note as a guiding principle for *the means of saying no with good faith.*

Warren Buffett has weighed in on the importance of saying no in career success. His advice goes like this:

> *Successful people say no to a lot of things.*
> *Really successful people, say no to almost everything.*

So, the art of "no" becomes a key to both career and investing success. As part of diversification, saying no is something that needs to be mastered to preserve focus. Remember that Warren Buffett and Bill Gates both said the key to success was in a single word: **FOCUS.**

By mastering the art of saying no, you provide yourself with the capacity to focus on maximizing both the quality and the margin of safety within a portfolio.

The absence of that discipline of saying no is one of the major issues for the investment-management business. Advisors have too many clients, and each client has too many individual holdings. Over time, those individual holdings build up in number to extraordinary levels. When one examines the investment holdings on the books of most investment advisors, there are thousands of individual investments.

It develops like this: an advisor builds a practice by building relationships with clients. As clients join the practice, they generally arrive with existing holdings. Sometimes they liquidate those in favor of the advisor's recommendations. Sometimes they elect to hold on to some of them going forward. People have their reasons: the time is not right to sell; the tax hit on sale is too much of a burden; they like the company, the management, the industry, etc.

Time passes. Hundreds of clients later, each client has a collection of a few individual securities or funds that were a legacy from other sources or that simply were not sold when the advisor recommended a change. The client can say no when the advisor recommends liquidation, but as long as the client holds the investment on the books, the advisor is still required to follow the security and ensure its suitability.

Most clients are over-diversified—often holding thirty (and even far more) portfolio holdings. If the practice has three hundred clients (a relatively modest number), and each client has just five legacy holdings, that is a total of 1,500 investments that the advisor is responsible to follow.

What is the probability of an advisor being able to competently stay abreast of a portfolio of 1,500 (and frequently more) individual investments? The answer is mathematically indistinguishable from zero. Zip. Nada. Bupkis. There is no way possible that any individual is capable of following hundreds of individual securities with due diligence, let alone thousands.

The regulators say: "Know your client and know your product." However, the reality is that for most advisors, the investment-practice reality is excessively diverse on both terms. As a result, both the advisor and the firm are open to liability for adverse results.

You want a successful advisor. You want a focused advisor. Find an advisor who has the discipline to say no.

Therein lies one differential factor between a competent advisor and a salesperson: the discipline to say no. Without it, the benefit of focus is lost.

But you also want a portfolio that you can stay focused on so that you can diligently manage it.

For a particularly well-written discussion of the importance of saying no, you might want to read the book by Greg McKeown titled *Essentialism, the Disciplined Pursuit of Less.*

PRACTICAL ART #6:
TRADE EXECUTION

The Issue: So Many Options and So Little Time

Full-service financial advisors, fiduciary investment counsellors, discount brokers, fintech, robo advisors, commission-free trading, Robinhood, Wealthsimple, Charles Schwab...

...and oh, so many undisclosed issues, from the minuscule to the perilous to the felonious—many of which can adversely impact your trading execution.

For example, in almost every market, there are market makers, specialists in the security that is traded "on the floor," which is now on a digital microchip. But there is a bid-ask spread, sometimes disclosed, sometimes not, and front running of your pending trade by high-frequency traders that can manipulate the market in milliseconds before your trade can be executed as exposed by Brad Katsuyama.

Brad Katsuyama of RBC was credited with being the whistleblower on the "front-running" of markets by high-frequency trading platforms. Michael Lewis wrote a book about it titled *Flash Boys*, and a movie titled *The Hummingbird Project* followed. This was a small peek at the conflicts of interest that are everywhere in financial markets.

Commission-free trading brings in a great deal of commercial volume. There, the commissions may range from minuscule to zero, but while the stated commissions may be zero, the trade is not free.

To quote from the RBC thought piece on the subject and a Wikipedia summary of the book available in detail here:[34]

---

34   See: https://thoughtleadership.rbc.com/flash-forward-flash-boys-canadian-shaking-wall-street/and https://en.wikipedia.org/wiki/Flash_Boys

"Stock exchanges are private, for-profit companies, and it's in their interests to make money by offering preferential access to high-frequency traders and anyone else who wants to pay for it. Some traders use this access to get an advantage, sniffing out big orders and racing to buy up the available stocks before the original order can be completed. This all happens in microseconds, far beyond the ability of any human to react. But for computers, such a task is trivial."

Brokerage firms enhance their revenue by receiving payments from exchanges for "order flow," where inbound trades are directed to specific exchanges in return for compensation from the originator. This is not a not-for-profit charitable function to benefit the client. It is an alternative form of cost that replaces the regular commission stream. Knowingly or not, it is the client that writes the cheque.

The Solution

Always use a fixed price limit on orders where the specialist in the security can provide the trade at that specific price *or on better terms if available.*

On the US markets, this is a common occurrence where your fill is at a market limit price that is better than the stated limit due to market conditions. In Canada, it is extremely rare for an order fill to be in favor of the buyer.

Enhanced Solutions

Like the Shaolin master counselled: "Patience, Grasshopper."

Place your orders on a fixed limit for an extended "Good Till" period so that the market volatility will work in your favor. There are many more strategies: executing the trade using option strategies to reduce your costs or, if large in volume,

VWAP (volume weighted average price); computer-driven execution; the list goes on. However, *these are not safe places for those without expert knowledge or serious commitment to the task.*

Always use a "fixed limit" price rather than a "market order," so you will not get a surprise and *The Flash Boys* are defeated.

PART E

Simplified Investment Process Examples

The following three investment process examples are not intended to be used as presented. They are simplified to provide examples as thought pieces. *The Dogs of the Dow* has been shown to successfully add value relative to the underlying Dow 30 as a benchmark providing excess returns in most years. *The Deals of the Dow* is a name that I have elected to utilize for a significantly simplified version of the North American portfolio I used in my former practice. *The Dangers* represents the opposite end of the relative valuation of the Deals: the ten most expensive members of the Dow 30 Industrials. It is shown so you will get a clear appreciation of how wide the variations are between market values and what the Graham Formula estimates to be intrinsic value. They should serve merely as a place to start in building your own investment process.

EXAMPLE #1:
THE DOGS OF THE DOW

"Dogs of the Dow" is an investment strategy that attempts to beat the Dow Jones Industrial Average (DJIA) each year by leaning portfolios toward high-yield investments. The general concept is to allocate money to the ten highest dividend-yielding, blue-chip stocks among the thirty components of the DJIA.

Jeremy Siegel endorses the Dogs of the Dow, describing it in *The Future for Investors* (2005) as "one of the most successful investment strategies of all time." The Dogs method can be particularly effective in adverse markets according to Siegel, as "dividends cushioned the declines in the market."

The evaluation of performance is mixed. Generally, it is believed the "Dogs" added value over the Dow performance over long periods, but it can underperform for shorter periods of several years also.

In the "Dogs of the Dow," simplicity is paramount, and the investment decision process is limited to an examination of which ten of the thirty stocks have *the highest dividend yields*. It is not what Graham would describe as "a thorough analysis" investing process. However, it is a process, it does add value, it removes emotion, and it does perform.

In the "Deals of the Dow," the math is slightly more complex. The investor examines what the growth in earnings will be for each security, calculates the intrinsic value using the Graham Formula, and then lists the entire thirty industrial issues sorted in order of *discount to intrinsic value* otherwise referred to as the margin of safety. The ten largest margins of safety (biggest discounts) are selected for potential investment, provided the market price represents a minimum one-third discount to intrinsic value. Independent evaluation of the performance is significantly better for the "Deals" than the "Dogs," with the added benefit of less risk of losses.

In absolute terms, the added return earned by the "Dogs of the Dow" is relatively insignificant compared with what follows next in "The Deals of the Dow.©"

EXAMPLE #2:
THE DEALS OF THE DOW©

The "Deals of the Dow" is a name of my own making. It is provided as a simplified example of how the Graham Formula works in practice. In support of the methodology is a seventeen-year research study that measured (1997–2013) the results of the Graham Formula. Applied in the manner that I use (a discount to the intrinsic value of one-third or more), the study concluded that the Graham Formula significantly outperformed the Dow both in absolute terms (more than twice the return) and risk-adjusted terms (seventeen years without a single down year). See Appendix E: Assessing the Graham Formula.

There are three sources of input for this example:

1. Individual Value Line© Research Reports.[35] The research source of the inputs is from Value Line, which generously provides on a complimentary basis their research covering the thirty stocks that comprise the Dow Jones Industrial Average updated quarterly.

2. The Deals of the Dow Spreadsheet (Appendix D). This relatively straightforward spreadsheet outlines the actual means by which the Graham Formula is used to focus an already concentrated universe of extraordinary businesses (with each possessing most of the characteristics of what makes a great business) into a group of great investment candidates. Great businesses are available for investment at a wide discount to their intrinsic value. As a subset of the Dow 30 universe of issuers, once an estimated present valuation of the future earnings has been calculated, the entire thirty issues can be sorted on the basis of the discount to intrinsic value. The ten

35   Readers can access that generous resource here: https://research.valueline.com/research#list=dow30&sec=list

issues that represent the largest margins of safety represent what I call "The Deals of the Dow."

3. Assessing the Graham Formula (Appendix E). As a portfolio manager, I used the Graham formula for twenty-five years with significant success and *no client complaints*. After retiring, the statistical success of this method as the subject of a research study was found as an independent confirmation of its validity.[36]

Upon examination of the Deals of the Dow© spreadsheet in Appendix D, the following items are points for examination by the reader:

- The sample spreadsheet was assembled, on April 14, 2023, using closing prices from the previous day, April 13, 2023.

- For the Dow 30 Industrials as a whole, the trailing price-earnings multiple was 19.1 times. That is relatively somewhat expensive. Extremely low-interest rates had served to expand asset values.

- When the ten most expensive issues are isolated as a group (the Dangers), the P/E jumps to over thirty-six times (an earnings yield of less than 3%), the earnings growth rate forecasted by the Value Line research reports stood at 20.8%, and the dividend yield stood at 1.4%. The expected return as a ten-stock portfolio would then be the total earnings growth (20.8%) plus dividend yield (1.4%) or 22.2% *before any potential contraction in the 36.5 times price-earnings multiple.*

- When the ten least expensive issues are isolated as a group, the relative metrics are:

  - Price to Earnings Multiple (P/E): Deals 15.2x (vs. Dangers 36.5)

---

36   See: https://file.scirp.org/pdf/JSS_2014030612000517.pdf

- Compound growth in earnings growth rate: Deals 13.0% (vs. Dangers 20.8%)
- Dividend yield: Deals 3.6% (vs. Dangers 1.4%)
- Total expected return: Deals (13.0% plus 3.6%) = 16.6% (vs Dangers 20.8 + 1.4 = 22.2%)

- *The differential factor here is the overall margins of safety.* For the Dow 30 as a group, the average indicates a discount from the intrinsic value of 22.1%. History teaches that when the Graham Formula indicates the market to be within 20% of the total intrinsic value, there is a significant risk of a general market correction. The "Deals of the Dow," the ten least expensive stocks in terms of the margin of safety discount, show an average discount from the intrinsic value of 57%. That implies that you can buy dollars for $0.43 cents. Comparatively, the ten most expensive issues are selling for a 19.5% premium over their intrinsic value, equivalent to buying dollars at a significant premium to what they are worth. As a group they have no margin of safety.

In my investment management practice, I used a larger universe of investment candidates. Following 120 to 150 companies requires considerable time to become intimately familiar with the individual businesses and a substantial amount of effort to maintain the database updated with earnings estimates as revised by Value Line. The "Deals of the Dow" is provided as a scaled-down version of my North American Large Capitalization Equity portfolio, which was run for clients in my practice.

The Deals model represents high-quality candidates meeting many of the five characteristics of great companies, particularly in terms of balance-sheet quality. They also have extensive research available free of charge from Value Line.

In the spreadsheet, the ten Deals stocks represent a very significant discount to their Graham Formula value estimates (57%), which is much larger than the Dow 30 stocks as an index 22.1% discount to Graham Formula value) and the ten Dangers most expensive stocks (19.5% overpriced).

Now that is investing as Graham defined it:

1. "A thorough analysis" (the practical applications above).
2. "Safety of principal" (a 57% margin of safety discount to value).
3. "An adequate return (for the "Deals" example of 16.6% *before any potential P/E multiple expansion*).

EXAMPLE #3:
THE DANGERS

"The Dangers" is the opposite application of the Deals. Instead of selecting the ten stocks that provide the largest discount from the Graham Formula estimate for intrinsic value, the ten stocks with the smallest discount (and in some cases a market price that is more than intrinsic value) are selected. They represent a significant reduction in the safety of capital (risk of loss). As a result, they are examples of issuers where the popular appeal of the companies to the market participants has resulted in their prices being bid up to a point that they have little or no investment merit, even though they are excellent businesses.

With each price increase, there is a corresponding decrease in investment merit.

In another look at Appendix D, you can see that there is a wide differential of valuation parameters between the ten least expensive (The Deals) and the ten most expensive (The Dangers) Dow components when viewed as individual ten stock portfolios. In the ten most expensive issues of the Dow 30 components, the relative **Compound Average Growth Rates (CAGR)** from the Value Line reports indicated at the time of production of the spreadsheet that the Deals had a projected earnings growth of 13.0%. That is slightly more than twice 6.3% of the Dogs and 62.5% of the Dangers.

The relative average dividend yield for the Deals is 3.6%, which is 82% of the Dogs and almost twice the 1.4% yield of the "Dangers."

The **Price Earnings Ratio** (P/E) for the three groups is substantially greater in the differential than the growth or yield metrics.

The Deals P/E of 15.2 times is just slightly less than 14% of the P/E of the Dangers which stood at 111 times.

The key metric here is not P/E or dividend yield. The key is the relationship to estimated intrinsic value.

The Deals portfolio is selling at a significant discount of 57% while the Dangers is selling at a premium of 19.5% to the Graham Formula value. With the Deals, you are buying dollars of value for $0.43 cents. With the Dangers, you are paying $1.20 for each dollar of value. That is roughly equivalent to attempting to drive a 12-ton truck over a bridge rated for ten tons (20,000 pounds). For me, I prefer buying dollars for dimes.

When I was a student, one of my finance professors felt that the expected return of an equity security could best be measured in the formula of the combined total of the growth in earnings and the dividend yield. For his purposes, the expected return of the two groups would be as follows:

Deals: 3.6% yield plus 13% growth; total expected return 16.6%.

Dangers: 1.4% yield plus 20.8% growth; total expected return 22.2%%.

That assumption has a caveat. The return expectation is before the impact of "reversion to the mean," sometimes called the most powerful force in the financial universe. In this case, the reversion is potentially driven by the price earnings multiple expanding or contracting to a normalized level. In the above case, that could be:

(1) a contracting of the 19.5% premium in the "Dangers" to the Graham Formula calculated value (1.195 to 1.0 is a 16% decline) and that would reduce the expected return from 22.2% to 18.6%.

(2) a potential expansion in the "Deals" multiple to the Graham Formula value, and the impact of that would be an increase from a discount of 57% to Graham Formula

value (from .43 to 1 is an increase of 2.3-fold) indicating an increase in the expected return from 16.6% to 38.6%.

(3) instead of a potential multiple contraction, substantially increased upside from a potential multiple expansion.

Ask which you would rather undertake as an investment expectation with all three factors considered: growth, yield, and multiple valuation changes.

Another model in finance class was earnings yield (the inverse of the P/E) plus growth rate. Relative values for the deals and dangers:

Deals: Earnings yield (1/15.2) =6.6% + 13% (EPS CAGR) = 19.6%

Dangers: Earnings yield (1/111) =0.1% + 20.8% (EPS CAGR) = 20.9%

Paying over 100 times earnings for stocks that have higher prospects of growth and less dividend yield is a risky path to travel because the probability of that growth is highly uncertain (remember the risks of forecasts). Paying slightly over fifteen times earnings for a portfolio expected to grow earnings at 13% while paying a dividend yield of 3.6% is a safer way to protect capital and earn acceptable returns. The impact of earnings failing to grow at forecasted rates is much lower when the multiple is lower.

Price is what you pay. Value is what you get.

Only buy quality when it is available at a discount to your estimate of intrinsic value.

A very successful neighbor who had built a large real-estate portfolio advised me as a young man that: "You get what you pay for; sometimes less, never more." Unfortunately, he was later caught in a downturn and his success did not endure.

The lessons of value investing in the stock market have taught me that while you sometimes can get what you pay for, you also sometimes (often) risk receiving significantly less in value than what you paid for in price. Despite those risks, there are sufficient opportunities that present themselves at times to acquire more in value than is asked for in price by the market quotations that result from irrational behavior of other market participants.

Key Takeaways

Market quotations provide prices. Price is what you pay.

Value is what you get.

The sum of future earnings is what provides value. Conservatively estimated and discounted for risk into present dollar values, they represent the intrinsic value of the investment.

Let the volatility of the price quotes serve you rather than direct you.

Knowledge and process provide the ability to know the difference between price and value, and therein lies the potential to find the crucial **margin of safety**.

EXAMPLE #4:
INVESTMENT POLICY IN PRACTICE

"The main reason why money is lost in stock speculation is not because Wall Street is dishonest, but because so many people persist in thinking that you can make money without working for it and that the stock exchange is the place where this miracle can be performed."

—Bernard Baruch

Bernard Baruch (1870–1965) was a lot of things: one of the wealthiest people of his time, an ambassador, and an advisor to US presidents over four decades. He is attributed as having been so repulsed by the speculative behavior of the late 1920s that when a shoeshine boy tried to give him stock advice, he cancelled his meetings, sold his investments, traveled with his wife to Europe for six months, and returned to the States after the crash of 1929. Asked how he made so much money in Wall Street he is said to have replied: "I sold too early."

Benjamin Graham (1894–1976) was younger than Baruch and was invited to join Baruch as a partner in his firm. Graham and Baruch both agreed the stock market in 1925 was marked by inexcusable excess and would be headed to a major crash. Graham later lamented he could see the risk and predict a crash but did not have the sense to realize the danger to his own accounts. Graham lost over 80% of his capital from 1929 to 1932. Baruch sold "too early" and avoided the resulting misfortune.

What follows are three short topics (some paraphrased) from Bernard Baruch's autobiography, BARUCH: *My Own Story*,[37] originally published in 1957. These include valuable wisdom on investment policy, investment knowledge, and the stock market. They are referenced because they are excellent examples of investment policy that are entirely as relevant today as they

---

37 *My Own Story*, Bernard Baruch, New York, Holt, Rinehart and Winston, 1957.

were when written more than a half century ago and practiced long before that.

Baruch: On Investment Policy[38]

1. Don't speculate (unless you make it a full-time job).
2. Beware... of "inside" information or "tips."
3. Before buying ...learn everything you can about the company: its management, competitors, earnings, and possibilities for growth.
4. Don't try to buy at the bottom and sell at the top. Only liars can do this.
5. Learn to take losses quickly and cleanly. You won't always be right. When you make a mistake, cut your losses quickly.
6. Don't buy many securities. Fewer investments that can be closely watched is better.
7. Periodically reappraise your investments to see if changing developments have altered their prospects.
8. Know when you can sell to the greatest tax advantage.
9. Always keep a good part of your capital in a cash reserve.
10. Don't try to be a jack of all trades in your investments. Stick to the field you know best.

---

38   Ibid., paraphrased from page 254 as an example of a simplified Statement of Investment Policy.

Baruch: On Investment Knowledge[39]

"In no field is the old maxim more valid—that a little knowledge is a dangerous thing—than in investing."

1. First, there are real assets of a company: the cash ... over its debt and what physical properties are worth.
2. Second, there is the (business) franchise..., which is another way of saying whether or not it makes something or performs a service that people want or must have.
3. Third, *and most important,* is the character and brains of management. Poor management can ruin even a good proposition.

Baruch: On the Stock Market[40]

It would be well to bear in mind two things:

First, the stock market does not determine the health of our economy... It is simply *a marketplace where buyers and sellers of securities meet.* All the market does is register the judgements of those sellers and buyers on what business is like and what it will be like in the future...

Second [is the] illusion that people can be protected against speculative losses through regulation...No law can protect a man from his own errors.

---

39 Ibid., 256
40 Ibid., Baruch pp. 263-264

PART F

Tactical Implementation of Investment Strategy

This section includes a summary of managing investment risk and capturing opportunity in the face of uncertainty; the constants of death, taxes, and human nature; and a few investing guidelines that are absolutes.

EIGHT PILLARS FOR MANAGING RISK AND THE CERTAINTY OF OUTCOMES

Managing Risk and Certainty of Outcomes

The following set of "Eight Pillars" is a foundation upon which to develop your own investment process guidelines. You have been introduced to the DOS questions from The Strategic Coach as a starting point to begin the development of your own "Building Blocks," starting with a written Statement of Investment Objectives, followed by a formal Financial Plan and finally a written Statement of Investment Policy. (See 1. a. to c. below.)

From there, a review of the Graham Formula study will serve as a starting point for simplifying the search for wide margins of safety and the development of your own process.

What follows are the "Building Blocks" upon which a personalized rational framework for making investment decisions can be constructed. A written Statement of Investment Objectives is the starting point, followed by a formal Financial Plan and then the development of an investment process, which is documented into a formalized Investment Policy Statement. From there, comes building a universe of candidates (as The Dream Team), and then a wide variety of research. The fundamental steps, as I see them, are laid out in the next set of eight "Pillars" to build on.

1. **The Objectives, the Plan, the Policy, the Process.**
   a) The Statement of Investment Objectives needs to be in written form developed in concert with the input of significant others. It also should be specific in amounts, priorities, and time horizons.
   b) The Financial Plan (many brokers include it for free)
   c) The Investment Policy Statement, which contains the written constraints of The Investment Process (the Graham Formula). (Keep it very

simple, keep it very close at hand, and refer to it before executing investment decisions.)

2. **The Universe of Investment Candidates (the Dream Team)**
   a) The Deals of the Dow,© for an example as a possible start.
   a) Expand the list using your knowledge and experience.
   b) Invest in companies you admire (the Peter Lynch example).
   c) Focus on the five characteristics of investment excellence.
   d) Understand their sustainable competitive advantages.
   e) Value Line is a worthwhile time-saving efficiency tool.

3. **Calculate Estimated Intrinsic Values (the Graham Formula)**
   a) Build a dream team spreadsheet that can evolve over time.
   b) Keep it simple and focused.

4. **Rank the Candidates for Consideration (Focus Further)**
   a) Build the equity portfolio from that small dream team universe.
   b) Review the candidates regularly (quarterly) as things evolve.

5. **Understand the Reason for the Discount to Intrinsic Value**
   a) Is it a temporary or a permanent change to prospects?

b) Identify potential catalysts to
impact market valuation.

6. **Confirm Your Assessment with Third-Party Sources**
   a) Insider Activity (Nasdaq) (are the insiders buying?)
   b) Analyst Ratings (do they see something you do not?)
   c) Analyst targets (best/worst case,
   assess risk and reward)
   d) Follow the leaders (Berkshire/
   Fairfax/Cascades 13G)

7. **Maximize both Quality and Safety
   (quality is always first)**

8. **Assess Your Performance (learn, adjust, adapt, repeat)**
   a) Review heroic intentions measured
   against realized results.
   b) Learn from both what does and what does not work.
   c) Amend your objectives, plan, policy, and process.
   d) Repeat.

CERTAINTY OF OUTCOMES AND MANAGEMENT OF PROBABILITIES

*The revolutionary idea that defines the boundary
between modern times and the past is the mastery of risk:
the notion that the future is more than the whim of the gods
and that men and women are not passive before nature.*

—Peter L. Bernstein, in *Against the Gods:
The Remarkable Story of Risk*

Fluctuations and Volatility

There are few certainties in market behaviors, except the fact stated by J. Pierpont Morgan when asked what the market would do: **"Stocks Will Fluctuate."**

Morgan's certainty of fluctuations in the market price quotations of securities is the volatility produced by the collective human behaviors of individual market participants. Today, humans have created algorithms to drive computer trades that can impact and sometimes add to that volatility.

Morgan was straightforward and very succinct in his comments. Modern finance is anything but in the use of terminology to describe risk. As a result, for the sake of clarity, the next few passages will be devoted to defining the terms of reference for what is being communicated. In the world of finance, there is an unsettling tendency to use the word "risk" as synonymous with "volatility." Let there be no misinterpretation of the intent here.

Intrinsic Value is an estimation of the present value of future earnings.

Management of Probabilities is the use of probability in one's behaviors to minimize (the risk of) loss and maximize the opportunity.

Opportunity is the possibility to achieve something.

Probability is the likelihood of a potential outcome occurring.

Risk is the possibility of a potential outcome being a loss.

Standard deviation is not risk. Standard deviation is the statistical measure of the probability associated with expected outcomes. It is a useful tool in the development of a response to events for the management of risk, but it is not risk itself.

Volatility is not risk. Volatility is the inherent tendency for change. That is what J.P. Morgan referred to when he said, "Stocks will fluctuate." It is what markets and economies do.

Markets are volatile. Stocks fluctuate. Market volatility presents risks and opportunities. Hence, it is no more appropriate to substitute the term "risk" for "volatility" than it would be to refer to "volatility" as an "opportunity." Risk appears when thinking is flawed. When an investor acts rationally, volatility is where opportunity may be found.

Chance favors the prepared mind.

Ben Franklin wrote: "…in this world nothing can be said to be certain, except death and taxes."

Heraclitus wrote that: "Nothing endures but change."

Machiavelli wrote: "Those who wish to see the future must consult the past; that historical events are produced by men, who ever have been, and ever will be, animated by the same passions: with the same results."

Conclusion: The enduring certainties are death, taxes, change, and human nature.

The human psychology of crowd behavior (that drives markets) is increasingly influenced by the reach and speed of communications. While situations are often reported inaccurately, dissemination is faster and broader with the Internet and social media, thus resulting in more volatility.

Now the good news: More volatility means both more risk for those who know not what they do and more opportunity for those with a prepared mind focused on process-driven investing in quality businesses when they are available for purchase at wide margins of safety.

30 DOW JONES INDUSTRIAL AVERAGE ISSUES 52 WEEK HI/LOW VOLATILITY

	DOW 30 INDUSTRIALS AVERAGE ISSUES	TICKER SYMBOL	CLOSING PRICE 22-Aug-23	52 WEEK HIGH	52 WEEK LOW	LOW TO HIGH	HIGH TO LOW
1	3M COMPANY	MMM	$98.51	$144.01	$92.38	55.9%	-35.9%
2	AMERICAN EXPRESS	AXP	$159.08	$182.15	$130.65	39.4%	-28.3%
3	AMGEN	AMGN	$257.62	$296.67	$211.71	40.1%	-28.6%
4	APPL	AAPL	$177.23	$198.23	$124.17	59.6%	-37.4%
5	BOEING	BA	$230.07	$243.10	$120.99	100.9%	-50.2%
6	CATERPILLAR	CAT	$270.20	$293.88	$160.60	83.0%	-45.4%
7	CHEVRON	CVX	$159.04	$189.68	$140.46	35.0%	-25.9%
8	CISCO	CSCO	$55.46	$56.20	$38.61	45.6%	-31.3%
9	COCA-COLA	KO	$60.06	$64.99	$54.02	20.3%	-16.9%
10	DOW INC	DOW	$53.79	$60.88	$42.91	41.9%	-29.5%
11	GOLDMAN SACHS	GS	$318.79	$389.58	$287.75	35.4%	-26.1%
12	HOME DEPOT	HD	$324.48	$347.25	$265.61	30.7%	-23.5%
13	HONEYWELL	HON	$186.01	$220.96	$166.63	32.6%	-24.6%
14	INTEL	INTC	$32.89	$37.19	$24.59	51.2%	-33.9%
15	IBM	IBM	$141.49	$153.21	$115.55	32.6%	-24.6%
16	JOHNSON & JOHNSON	JNJ	$166.02	$181.04	$150.11	20.6%	-17.1%
17	JP MORGAN CHASE	JPM	$146.38	$159.38	$101.28	57.4%	-36.5%
18	MCDONALD'S	MCD	$280.31	$299.35	$230.58	29.8%	-23.0%
19	MERCK	MRK	$107.23	$119.65	$84.52	41.6%	-29.4%
20	MICROSOFT	MSFT	$322.46	$366.78	$213.43	71.8%	-41.8%
21	NIKE	NKE	$101.46	$131.31	$82.22	59.7%	-37.4%
22	PROCTOR & GAMBLE	PG	$151.83	$158.38	$122.18	29.6%	-22.9%
23	SALESFORCE	CRM	$200.76	$238.22	$126.34	88.6%	-47.0%
24	TRAVELERS	TRV	$159.94	$194.51	$149.65	30.0%	-23.1%
25	UNITED HEALTH	UNH	$492.34	$558.10	$445.68	25.2%	-20.1%
26	VERIZON	VZ	$33.20	$44.13	$31.25	41.2%	-29.2%
27	VISA	V	$240.57	$245.37	$174.60	40.5%	-28.8%
28	WALGREENS	WBA	$26.54	$42.29	$26.12	61.9%	-38.2%
29	WALT DISNEY	DIS	$85.79	$118.37	$84.07	40.8%	-29.0%
30	WALMART	WMT	$157.01	$162.78	$128.07	27.1%	-21.3%
	AVERAGE 52 WEEK % CHANGE					45.7%	-30.2%

Market prices fluctuate widely, but future cashflows representing Intrinsic Values, do not fluctuate anywhere near that widely.

Consider looking at the volatility of the thirty securities that comprise the Dow Jones Industrial Average in the following table. The annual volatility in market price is demonstrated by the 52-week high and low figures in two ways; from low to high (an average of 46.1%) and from high to low (an average of 30.5%) with much wider swings in individual issue prices.

From the 52-week low to the 52-week high, the spread ranges between 20.3% and 100.9%. At the time of writing, this represents a current average percentage change in 52 weeks for the thirty issues in the Dow Jones Industrial Average of a 45.7% upside from low to high. And this is just in a single 52-week period!

From the 52-week high to the 52-week low, the declines represent a range of 16.9% to 50.2% with the average being 30.2%

This reality of volatility makes the concept of an efficient market seem more than a little erroneous. You can view this either as risk (if you buy at the high) or opportunity (if you buy at the low). You need to determine if your glass is half full or your glass is half empty. Hence the beginning of the counsel of this book: *First and foremost, know yourself.*

My standard counsel to clients in my practice was this: "The first thing that any stock I buy for you will do is go down, and the first thing that any stock that I sell for you will do is go up. You will not get in at the bottom nor will you get out at the top."

The reality that you cannot get the timing perfect does not prevent seeking to buy low and to sell dear from being worth the effort. The potential rewards are substantial. Those rewards can be realized best by those in possession of a prepared mind that executes a rational framework (read *investment policy*) for making investment decisions and relies on process to help prevent emotions from eroding it.

A Margin of Safety and the Graham Formula

Benjamin Graham offered a straightforward and simple formula to evaluate stocks' intrinsic value. Many regard the Graham Formula as a very simplistic way of measuring an individual company's intrinsic value. Graham and Warren Buffett, however, felt that the simplicity of the model allowed them to quickly and accurately identify undervalued companies and stay away from overvalued ones.

—*Jason Lin & Jane Sung, in* "Assessing the Graham Formula for Stock Selection: Too Good to be True?"

In my practice, to arrive at an acceptable "margin of safety," the estimated discount of market price to intrinsic value must be wider than one-third or 33%. That equates to a 1.5 times "Relative Graham Valuation" in the above-quoted study of Graham's Formula when inverted. That study demonstrated, over its seventeen-year term, that the formula produced a track record with not a single year of negative return and a cumulative return that was more than twice that of the underlying Dow 30 Industrial Average 30-stock universe from which the stock portfolio was selected.

A few words of caution:

First, the Graham Formula is not to be used in place of the role of analysis of the underlying enterprises, but rather *as a starting point to assemble a small subset of businesses worthy of that analysis.*

Second, it has been quoted from studies of human behavior that 85% of drivers consider their driving skills to be above average. This clearly is an example of flawed reasoning, combined with human nature and its tendency towards conceit.

In the world of investing, individuals make investment decisions in the hope that they will add value in their active investment activities, which will surpass the expected returns from passive investing in things like the Warren Buffett recommendation of a Standard & Poor's 500 index fund. Yet 90% of active investors underperform the results that they would have achieved had they invested personally as Buffett suggested. For 90% of readers, most would be better served if they focused on buying and holding a tax-efficient and fee-efficient index fund. **Unless the reader is prepared to undertake the analysis required to properly assess the investment candidate beyond the Graham Formula calculation, they should follow Buffett's advice and save themselves the effort and the risks involved in pursuing the enterprising investor's goal of enhanced performance.**

Third, the Graham Formula is not without its flaws: one of which is the impact of dividend policy. Consider two identical companies, except for the dividend policy. One pays 50% of its earnings out to shareholders. The other reinvests the earnings and pays no dividend. The second company will have a higher growth rate in earnings because of an enhanced compounding of shareholder capital. Yet in all other aspects, they are equal and should, to a private purchaser, be of equal value. But the Graham Formula affords the zero-dividend company a significantly higher valuation.

If one reinvests the dividends into the purchase of additional shares, abstracting from taxation, the result would be the same. Therefore, it makes sense to amend the formula to include the dividend yield as an enhancement to the growth rate so that companies are evaluated on a comparable (dividends reinvested) valuation basis.

The alternative to the Graham Formula is to perform a formal **DCF (discounted cash flow analysis)** to arrive at a valuation. You can do that, but I am with Buffett when he said in a recent interview: "I don't do discounted cash flow analysis."

Approximately correct is better than precisely wrong.

In Roman times, when engineers built a bridge, the quality-control methodology used was to have the builders and engineers stand under the bridge as the legions drove over it with chariots above their heads. Buffett makes an analogy to the margin of safety being like driving a 10,000-pound truck over a bridge built to carry 10,000 pounds. You can do it, but he would prefer a wider margin of safety.

Either a much lighter truck or a much stronger bridge is needed.

Investing with a margin of safety (based in the calculation of intrinsic value) satisfies Graham's definition of investing.

As Graham defined it, *"An investment operation is one which upon thorough analysis promises safety of principal[41] and an adequate return. Operations not meeting these requirements are speculative."*

---

41 In my opinion, the concepts of investment quality together with margin of safety are what provide for safety of principal and what also enhance the probability of realization of an adequate return.

The Importance of Quality

My advice to analysts would be to limit your appraisals to enterprises of investment quality, excluding from that category such as do not meet specific criteria of financial strength.
—Benjamin Graham

If you are dealing only with companies that possess defined characteristics of quality, the probability of a successful outcome is enhanced.

If you are dealing with valuations with a wide margin of safety, the probability of a successful outcome is also enhanced. You are buying dollars of future earnings at significant discounts to what they are worth today in terms of present value. The concept is easy to retain if you think of it as simply as "buying dollars for dimes." But these are not just ordinary dollars. These are much higher quality dollars due to the sustainable competitive advantages that the quality characteristics of the companies generating that cash flow possess. The probability of the outcome has increased in terms of certainty twice: first due to the quality of the investment and second because of the price at which it was acquired.

Heraclitus said the only thing that is constant is change.

Enterprises that have the financial capacity to withstand the challenges of adversity have a sustainable competitive advantage provided by their financial strength. When their weaker competitors succumb to adversity, they have the opportunity to profit from the misfortune of their competitors and gain market share, emerging even stronger. Companies and their fortunes rise and fall.

All investments can fall in price. The strongest ones will return while the weaker may cease to exist.

Certain Principles Are Fundamental Absolutes

First absolute: A security will not be considered for investment unless it is available at a margin of safety that represents a discount to the estimate of intrinsic value by *at least 33%.*

The implication for this allows for being approximately right in one's calculations. Better to be approximately correct than precisely wrong.

Second absolute: The portfolio *will hold no more than ten issues.*

The first reason for this is "focus." Every security in your portfolio is deserving of due diligence in its evaluation and monitoring. Every additional issue being followed reduces the effective focus of investment management and hence increases the risk of error.

To optimize your focus, you need to recognize your capacity limitations.

The second reason is that the benefits of diversification, while real, are largely realized with very small numbers of five (80%) to ten (96%) securities. Beyond that, there is the very little marginal benefit of diversification but a significant loss of focus. Remember that the key to success is, in the words of Buffett and Gates focus not diversification.

The "art" comes into play when deciding between the highest quality candidates that qualify, and those with the largest margins of safety. The goal is to simultaneously maximize both the quality and the margins of safety of the overall portfolio.

Third absolute(s): Three additional crucial factors should be assessed.

1. Understand the reason for the discount in price.

2. Determine if the cause is due to a temporary issue or if the business franchise is permanently damaged due to reputation, disruption, or other causes.
3. Identify a catalyst that is likely to result in the temporary valuation discount being reappraised.

Fourth absolute: Quality comes first, discount second. Every day the intelligent investor is faced with a choice:

Buy Company A that rates on a quality scale of 3 out of 5 at a margin of safety of 60% or,

Buy Company B, rating 4 out of 5 in quality, with a margin of safety of 40%.

Which should you choose? The better company or the wider margin of safety? That which maximizes the portfolio quality reduces the portfolio margin of safety. Deciding between the two probabilities is where the art comes into the process.

I offer this as a solution: In my world of actual portfolio practice, the issues of extraordinary quality are largely rarely available at the widest margins of safety. This can be resolved in the construction of what might be termed as the "dream team" of issuers, for example, the Deals of the Dow discussed earlier and in Appendix D.

With the universe of investment candidates selected for consideration (your own personal "dream team"), you have addressed the first of two steps: investment quality. Now comes the selection of the individual portfolio components based on discounts to intrinsic value. The Graham Formula produces a subset of the eligible candidates under consideration to be acquired at a significant discount to intrinsic value—that is, with wide margins of safety.

The easy lifting has now been completed. Now comes the heavy lifting. You need to evaluate your understanding of the reason for the discount from intrinsic value: whether the discount is due to a temporary issue or if the discount is there because of a permanent impairment of business prospects.

Finally, you need to identify the likelihood (probability management) of a catalyst to change the situation and result in a repricing of the security in the market to reflect more closely that calculated intrinsic valuation.

Consider what confidence interval you assign to the probability of your estimates. They are, after all, just estimates. That is why you want *wide* margins of safety. As the quantity and quality of opportunities increase (and the margin of safety increases), so do confidence limits for the probability of estimates. But when investment opportunities are easily found in abundance, it will be because markets conditions are difficult.

Buffett was greatly influenced by Graham and later by Munger. Munger in turn was more influenced by Phil Fisher (*Common Stocks, Uncommon Profits*). In *The Einstein of Money: The Life and Timeless Wisdom of Benjamin Graham*, author Joe Carlen states that Morningstar, a financial research company, described Philip Fisher's investment approach in one sentence: "Purchase and hold for the long term a concentrated portfolio of outstanding companies with compelling growth prospects that you understand very well."

My only modification of that approach is to start building a small universe of outstanding companies (there are not that many) and get to the point where you know them very well. Identify those with wide margins of safety when they periodically become available for acquisition at a discount. Perform your analysis on them and identify both the reasons for the discount and the catalysts for change. Then deploy your capital to build your focused portfolio.

Making the final choices for your investment involves balancing the level of quality against the size of the discount (quality vs.

price). This is where the ART of portfolio management practice comes into play: *simultaneously maximizing both the quality and the margins of safety.*

In my experience, one useful differentiating factor in today's world is an indicator that has never received mentioned outside of my practice. It is how a company manages human resources and the quality of management character. It is the ultimate arbiter in the evaluation of investment quality. Thorndike, in *The Outsiders*, provides a case study of what makes for exceptional management in terms of creating extraordinary value for shareholders.[42] I highly recommend reading it and using the examples of those management track records and unique personality traits as a guiding light for your own assessments. When the balance of quantifiable issues is close, reversion to the analysis of management character will simplify probability management.

If you do not trust the character of management, no degree of discount from intrinsic value can be sufficient to warrant capital being placed at risk.

You cannot make a good deal with a bad person.

---

42   *The Outsiders: Eight Unconventional CEOs* by William Thorndike, Jr. (Harvard Business Review Press, 2012), provides a case study of what makes for exceptional management in terms of creating extraordinary value for shareholders. I highly recommend reading it and using the examples of those management track records and unique personality traits as a guiding light for your own assessments.

TAXES

The second of the two certainties in this world: death and taxes.

This is a chapter that most readers might want to skip for it is difficult for most people to get excited about the subject of taxes unless they seek a means of simply paying less. A little context for those who continue reading. When I decided that getting my CPA would be a good career choice, so I could read a balance sheet properly, the practice of taxes was not on my priority list. But the work at my then-employer, Peat Marwick and Co. in Portland, Maine, was basically of two parts: audit or tax. Taxation was for me, far more interesting and, as time progressed, would turn out to be far more useful.

This led to an unforeseen strategic benefit, as many things in life tend to do. To convert my newly printed CPA into the Canadian equivalent of CA (Chartered Accountant back then, CPA now), additional proficiency needed to be demonstrated in Canadian tax and law. As a result of those studies, the opportunity arose to teach Canadian Income Taxation every Monday night at Acadia University for the winter semester. It was not the ideal time slot, so I taught the course along the lines of my undergraduate constitutional law professor Barclay MacMillan using the Socratic method.

Roll the clock again, this time fourteen years forward, and my phone rang with a former student who was kind enough to look me up just to tell me that she wanted me to know that of all her four years of classes at Acadia, my tax course was the best experience she had.

Add another sixteen years to the calendar: another CA who filled in for one of my lectures while I had to travel for my primary job came to me at a charitable fundraiser that we were both attending. He was kind enough to pull me aside to thank me and tell me that the Acadia University tax lecture experience thirty years earlier had a profound impact on the rest of his career. He so enjoyed the teaching experience that he spent the next thirty years focused on teaching as a supplement to his accounting practice.

So, taxes turned out to have unexpected upsides for my career, for people whose paths I crossed, and for the three tax audits I experienced in my career where the government ended up writing me the cheque, not the reverse.

One unfortunate objective that occasionally comes to the surface in some individuals is a myopic desire to leave this world "owing the tax man." I would rather spend my time in the company of individuals who have the goal of wanting to leave this world a better place. That is one of the two key perks in portfolio management: the opportunity to work with people you admire.

Given that it is only through the ordered functioning of society that we can have the large sea of opportunities upon which we are all afloat, personal taxes—like personal health, fitness, and hygiene—are a basic function of life to be attended to and streamlined. The mantra to my clients on the subject of income tax was and remains quite simple:

"I have no problem paying my taxes so long as I'm not paying yours."

The purpose of this chapter is to provide some assistance in making it easier for each of us to pay our respective share of tax—no more, no less.

This is where one of the benefits of the formal Financial Plan can be best realized: in minimizing the burden of taxes we each must bear.

First is the prerequisite of saving for the future. Depending on the circumstances, use those savings to reduce the tax burden: the tax-free benefits of tax-free savings accounts (TFSA in Canada and ROTH IRA in the US), the tax deferral afforded through retirement savings (RRSP in Canada and 401K in the US) and pensions plans, as well as life insurance policies.

The second is to structure your affairs in a tax-efficient manner. For the entrepreneurs, incorporate to get the small-business tax rate, capital gains exemption, and the ability to split incomes to lower the marginal rates while ensuring that personal income maximizes eligibility for government entitlement programs (CPP in Canada and Social Security in the US).

Third, once the financial capacity has been achieved to be independent, structure a charitable giving program that will reduce the current tax burden through the donation of appreciated securities when markets provide the opportunity to make dispositions free of capital gains being taxed. Donating the appreciated security effectively allows you to keep in tax refunds what would have been the equivalent of the tax-free half of the gain.

The province of Nova Scotia is selected for this example. The reason for selecting Nova Scotia is because it is here that the household-income level is near the lowest of income levels in the country, and the province stands with the one of highest marginal tax rate in Canada at 54%. This is before considering payroll or consumption taxes, which brings the marginal income tax burden to well over 60%. This is relatively extreme by most any standard of comparison. In most of the Unites States, the income is higher, and the tax rate is lower, so financial independence is generally more easily achieved (except for medical costs), with wider variations from state to state in America than between provinces in Canada.

The current average household income in Nova Scotia stands at an official level of approximately $80,000 (Statistics Canada, 2019). Split between two family members, the tax burden is approximately $8,923 (Wealthsimple website calculation: Federal $3,240, Provincial $2,970, Payroll $2,713).

Maximize the RRSP contribution in year one (40,000 x 18% = $7,200) and one saves $2,194, reducing the tax burden from $8,923 to $6,729. Continuing for twenty years along with maximum TFSA contributions and every individual has the capacity of accumulating more than a $1 million net worth by age seventy, even if they start at the age of fifty. That is a lot of saving; 18% of earned income into an RRSP and, at today's contribution room rate limits, an additional 15% ($6,000) into a TFSA.

A two-person household with an average income of $80,000 ($40,000 each) still has a combined after-tax household cash flow of $40,000 ($80,000 less $39,658, comprised of taxes of $13,458, contributions to the RRSP of $14,200 and TFSA of $12,000 =) $40,342 to spend on the necessities of life. The combined savings ($14,200 + $12,000=) $26,200 annually will compound to $1,000,000 over twenty years at an interest rate of 6.34%.

We live in a society that recognizes the need to provide for one's financial future. There are basic tools that are provided and, as one accumulates more means, there are more sophisticated, completely legal, and socially responsible means of protecting one's earnings and capital wealth.

The basics tools are:

- The Tax-Free Savings Account in Canada and the Roth IRA in the US.

- The RRSP in Canada and the 401K plan in the US.

- Defined Benefit and Defined Contribution Pensions.

For the more sophisticated:

- Privately controlled small-business corporations with eligible active business income.

- Individual pension plans the investor can design for themselves for those with active business income.

- Whole-life insurance policies, which can shelter excess capital from creditors, markets, and taxes.

Then there are fundamental planning techniques that can optimize the effective tax rates:

- Buying quality investments with strong economics that can compound earnings at above-average rates for long periods and defer capital gains (think Berkshire Hathaway or better still read the annual letters to shareholders from Warren Buffett, CEO)

- Harvesting tax losses to shelter realized gains.

- Donating appreciated securities to charity and eliminating the tax on the gain while simultaneously benefiting from charitable contribution tax credits and doing good for the community at the same time.

The above investment strategies require discipline to implement properly, and they just scratch the surface of what are ethical, legal, and available options for individual investors.

For a more detailed application to your situation, there is a financial-advisor industry that works in concert with tax accountants, corporate attorneys, financial planners, and chartered life underwriters. Seek out those professionals appropriate for your situation.

To know that you are getting the right advice from advocates, I might be able to assist. For readers who want to begin a dialogue, contact me at: iAdvocacy@icloud.com

No matter how much you have or earn, there is always someone who has more (except perhaps for Elon Musk in 2022). But there is always a faster crowd. The reverse is also true. Regardless of how much you think you need; you can always make ends meet on less. The vast majority of humanity (8 billion people) exists on a small fraction of North Americans' incomes (average world income <$10,000). In the example provided, 50% of the population makes more, and 50% makes less.

It is a question of choice and having the personal discipline to spend less and save more. Investment merit must drive the decision process rather than taxes.

Alan Bruce wrote a biography of Roy Jodrey, a Nova Scotian business icon who long ago passed. Roy had a simple formula for financial success that Allan Bruce succinctly quoted. I call it the Roy Jodrey diet:

"If you want to be thin don't eat. If you want to be rich, don't spend."

RISK

Risk comes from not knowing what you are doing.

—Warren Buffett

In my world, there are two broad kinds of risk: (1) errors of commission and (2) everything else. In the first, "errors of commission" are decisions you made where you were wrong. While that will happen a lot, to be successful you only need to be right more often than you are wrong.

It will help if you keep your errors small and allow your successful decisions to compound over long periods. Recognize your mistakes early and cut your losses quickly. More importantly, learn from them. Mistakes are the greatest teachers you will ever have if you learn from their lessons.

Risk mitigation of errors can be helped by several things:

- If you recognize the error early, the loss can be minimized.

- The fewer decisions you make, the fewer times you are exposed to committing an error.[43]

- Having a defined process and a small circle of competence with defined limits that you stay within, reduces the areas where you can make mistakes.

- Finally, turn the loss into an opportunity for learning or as my father would ask me when I made a mistake: "Did you learn anything from that?"

For example, the third-generation asset management firm Davis Advisors in New York had a "wall of shame" where

---

43   "You only have an opinion on a few things. In fact, I've told students if when they got out of school, they got a punch card with 20 punches on it, and that's all the investment decisions they got to make in their entire life, they would get very rich because they would think very hard about each one."-*Warren Buffett's 20-hole punch card strategy from a talk delivered at Georgetown University September 19, 2013.*

share certificates of investments that did not work as planned are framed and mounted on a "wall of mistakes" with a small caption under each as to the lesson learned.

Lessons in humility: In 1981, a former neighbor in Connecticut moved to Prince Edward Island. As an aspiring young private pilot, I flew to PEI to visit him and, over lunch with a pen and a paper placemat, he introduced me to a firm in Omaha, Nebraska run by Warren Buffett.

He made a strong case, and it sounded like a good idea. But when he told me the shares were $2,300, I failed to recognize the value. Roll the clock forward ten years to 1991. Berkshire Hathaway is the largest shareholder of Coke and the "New Coke" had been received poorly. The same Berkshire Hathaway shares that had grown more than four-fold, fell from $10,000 to $5,000. Having just bought a new house, I again passed on investing. I was now compounding errors of omission.

Those shares are now over US$500,000 each. No commissions, fees or taxes would have been paid in the intervening thirty years.

- $2,300 in 1981 to $500,000 in 2022 (41 years) is a gain of 14.0% per year.
- $5,000 in 1991 to $500,000 in 2022 (31 years) is a gain of 15.7% per year.

You can't frame share certificates you never owned. Nonetheless, that one failure deserves special mention on my personal, long wall of errors.

Errors of omission are entirely another area of risk. Lost opportunity from what might have been is a much larger universe of risk than errors of commission. The only tool that I can offer to protect against errors of omission is to look at every situation, especially in the case of adversity, and ask one simple question: "Where's the opportunity?"

As politician and diplomat Rahm Emanuel has repeatedly said: "Never let a crisis go to waste."

Focusing on what could have been, other than to learn from that mistake, is unhealthy and unproductive. It is never a good idea to "should" on yourself. The "would have," "could have," "should have" of life accomplishes nothing other than destroying one's confidence.

As for all the other kinds of risk, the subjects are beyond the scope of this book.

Have the courage of your convictions to act.

CONCLUSION

The Madness of Crowds

"Men, it has been said, go mad in herds,
while they only recover their senses slowly, and one by one."
—Charles MacKay, *Memoirs of Extraordinary Popular Delusions and*
the Madness of Crowds

Behavioral Psychology

People tend to extremes in behavior, especially in crowds. The introduction of social-media technology into society is offered as modern case study. A defined investment process and investment policy will protect from risky behavior, but it will not eliminate it. Investment decision makers are continuously confronted with emotional triggers. "Emotional discipline" is possible to be supported by using policy and process in the decision process to replace emotion, but the underlying disciplined temperament must first be provided by the investor. If emotion is the biggest obstacle to investment success, the investor's largest generator of opportunity lies in emotional market-participant behaviors that misprice security issues.

It is, however, better to have the *actual opportunity* presented by market circumstances, whereby a price has been marked down below its intrinsic value by market events, than to rely on the hope that some *future eventual possibility* (i.e., increased earnings, a takeover, improving conditions) might result in the price rising higher than it is now. Another way of looking at that reality is to say that you make your profit when "buying right" rather than through the timing of selling. If you patiently wait for a real opportunity to be presented cheaply (the fat pitch), your patience will almost certainly be rewarded. There is much uncertainty in investing through hopeful optimism about what might someday be.

Long-Term Multigenerational Benchmarks

Ownership of "the market" will, in the absence of trading costs and emotional turnover, return 8% to 10% annually over a market cycle that tends to be about thirty years long. If you can invest into the market at the bottom once every thirty years, the results will be even better. If you invest once in thirty years at the top, the results will be worse. The market conditions of the day will have a large impact on passive strategy.

The relative valuations of the market can be viewed from a historical perspective. For instance, there was the "Internet bubble," which was characterized by behavioral excess; the recent real-estate cycle; and the recent and previous gold bubbles. Any investment that has received broad acceptance is an investment that has significant inherent danger because the buyers have already all bought. Once the tide turns, there will be no buyers left, only sellers.

Tactical Asset Allocation

It's appropriate to be cautious when it's clear that large numbers of individuals are behaving in a cavalier manner toward risk. You can adjust to the degrees accordingly. But courage in asset allocation will be rewarded when there is pessimism regarding prospects resembling mass emotional depression. "Be fearful when others are greedy, and greedy when others are fearful," Buffett warns us. "Buy to the sound of cannons, sell to the sound of trumpets," is attributed to Baron de Rothschild.

A small amount of asset-allocation flexibility in the Investment Policy Statement, a minimum of plus or minus 10%, can greatly enhance returns if applied in a timely manner.

Ben Graham said, "You're never all right or all wrong." His advice on asset allocation was to take 50% of your capital and divide it between stocks and bonds. Take the other half and place it where you perceive the greatest risk/reward to exist." That means you could be as much as 75% in the market or as little as 25%, depending on the expectations for the markets and the relative attractiveness of opportunities.

Keep in mind that you must attentively watch the behavior of market participants and be careful not to follow the crowd.

Cyclical Variations and Reversion to the Mean

The business cycle, in varying degrees, is as sure as the cycle of the seasons. It can be measured and seen in the readily available published economic statistics, but to see it in context requires discipline and a keen, observant eye. Like a sailor in bygone days who would watch the changes in the sky and wind, keep an eye on the seasons, and pay regular attention to the barometric pressure changes. You will be able to eliminate much uncertainty by observing the general trend of human behavior towards risk.

The single most powerful force in economics is said to be "reversion to the mean." It is not palpable, but it is certain. When you limit your focus to a small subset of investments, you're more likely to notice variances from normal values. When they shift in one direction, you can be certain that they will eventually return to the mean. Keep a weather eye on the changes that occur around you, and you'll perceive the nearly imperceptible. The rewards will go to those who keep a watchful eye on what others choose to blissfully ignore at their peril. There is a quote that illustrates this very well in the November 6, 2010, issue of *The Economist:* "Subtle gravitational shifts of the moon are imperceptible to humans, yet they are able to move oceans multiple times each day."

Some people say that you make money when you buy properly, not when you sell. Other people say you make money owning assets over time and not buying and selling. Either way can work but combining them can be better.

We live in a time of accelerating change. Long-term holdings can be tax efficient, but the creation of wealth is maximized by letting quality and margins of safety drive the investment decision rather than issues of taxation. Passive investment strategies can incur a significantly larger price in performance and eventual capital destruction than the small amounts of transaction costs saved and interest on taxes deferred. Management of investment assets requires ongoing diligence. This is even more so today than in prior periods, as the rate of change and innovation in modern times accelerates along with the advancement of the technical complexities of our society.

The Weather Eye

> *Keep a weather eye to the chart on high*
> *and go home another way.*
>
> —James Taylor

Equity returns have averaged approximately 8.5% over the last 200 years with significantly more of that return being derived from dividends in the past than is available today. As interest rates today are well below the levels that history would suggest are normal, there is little basis to expect that dividends will be driven higher by market conditions any time soon. So, it becomes important that the investor have expectations as to returns that are reasonable in light of market conditions. You can adopt a passive strategy, forgo the effort required to actively manage your portfolio within the constraints of an appropriate investment policy, and still achieve positive results. The extra effort to go beyond the present-day fashion for indexing presents the opportunity to significantly reward those efforts. Not so for the majority, but those who choose to walk a different path, armed with a disciplined process developed from an articulated investment policy—they "go home by another way."

In Appendix F, the miracle of compound interest is demonstrated in the first of two spreadsheets, "The 3% Difference: The difference 3% makes in cumulative returns over forty years."

Each column assumes a beginning capital value of $100,000 and a forty-year, long-term time horizon. In the first column, the forty years represent the approximate investing time horizon between becoming established in the workforce full-time (age twenty-five) and retirement (age sixty-five).

The first "Account" column values use an expected base rate of return of 7%. It is a typical return assumption for a balanced exchange-traded fund portfolio on a 40/60 allocation of stocks and bonds. Terminal value is $1.5 million.

The second "Account" column then uses an assumption of a 10% return that is chosen to demonstrate the "3% Difference" that an actively managed equity portfolio might achieve. Terminal value is $4.5 million.

The end value is three times more because of a 3% additional return.

The second spreadsheet, "Results of Differential Rates of Return," uses a real-world return assumption of 12.07% representing the actual return of the S&P 500 over the past twenty years compared to the compounding rate of the book value of Fairfax Financial Holdings of 18.2% from inception when Prem Watsa became CEO in 1985 until 2021 (thirty-six years).

The terminal value of the original $100,000 grows to $7.4 million over forty years when compounded at 12.07%, the actual S&P 500 total return for the past twenty years. This is compared with a second column representing the actual compound rate of growth of 18.2% in the book value of Fairfax Financial Holdings over the past thirty-six years from the 2021 annual report to shareholders.

Those rates of return are extrapolated into a forty-year time horizon. The corresponding returns realized over the comparable thirty-year period for the market value of Berkshire Hathaway are nearly identical to that of Fairfax for comparable periods.

The terminal value for the S&P 500 return of 12.1% is $9.5 million. Terminal value for the same beginning $100,000 sum compounded at Fairfax Financial rate of return of 18.2% reaches a terminal value of $80.3 million.

A little extra return makes a very large difference over extended periods. That is the miracle of compounding.

Yes, diligently watch the costs (of commissions, fees, and taxes), but keep them in perspective over the impact on the long-term results.

Spend most of your time and effort on selecting the quality of the business: its long-term sustainable competitive advantages to enable high returns on invested capital; the quality, integrity, and motivational incentives of its management; and the margin of safety in the price.

AFTERWORD

First, get the building blocks right:

- A written Statement of Investment Objectives

- A formal written Financial Plan that establishes targets and timelines

- A tailored Investment Policy Statement that will provide an anchor when the markets swing to excesses; it should define asset allocation targets and the investment process and include monitoring actual results against intentions.

Second, get the investment process right and continually refine it.

- Build a small, focused universe of exceptional (Dream Team) companies that meet the five criteria for great businesses from which to select potential investments.

- Only commit to deploying your capital when you can acquire those shares at wide margins of safety because they are available to purchase at substantial discounts to your conservative estimate of their intrinsic values.

- Focus on your investment portfolio so that you can follow it closely by limiting the total number of decisions you make. The vast majority of the wealth created by Berkshire Hathaway was achieved by eight investment decisions in its first fifty years.

Third, consider the wisdom of Solomon:

- Be diligent in your efforts.
- Seek out wisdom and wise counsel wherever you can find it.
- Protect your confidence by surrounding yourself with good people.

Finally, there is something new afoot in the neighborhood.

- There is a long-standing market adage that says the four most dangerous words on Wall Street are: "This time is different." The reason it is so well known for its cautionary wisdom is that the fundamentals of markets are, in turn, the fundamentals of human behavior, which does not change over time. As a result, all the "new" investment concepts eventually turn out to be a variation on old themes designed to drive sales.
- *"But perhaps the world has changed, and as I grew old, I failed to see it."*[44] As I complete this manuscript, I can share with you my pleasure at having just read a book that might be one of the best investing books I have had the pleasure of reading in a long time. Adam Sesseel breaks down his three-staged assessment of value investing into Value Investing 1.0 (Ben Graham); 2.0 (Warren Buffett and Value); and 3.0 the BMP Checklist (**B**usiness, **M**anagement, **P**rice). Although he does not address intrinsic value or the Graham Formula, he does a very good job of identifying what was fundamental in the past and his own version of determining pricing power in the evaluation of platform and network-based businesses in the age of the microprocessor-induced revolution we all live in today. If you are a fan of the

44   Adam Seessel, in his new book *Where the Money Is*, Avid Reader Press, 2022

potential of companies that operate in the digital environment like Alphabet, Amazon, Intuit, or Microsoft, etc., then it is a very interesting read.

So, to quote Churchill: "This is not the end. This is not even the beginning of the end, but it may just be the end of the beginning." *From here, you have an opportunity, to think about investing differently than you have previously.*

It is time to begin your own journey in the development of an individualized investment-management process. To do this, articulate your Investment Objectives, quantify your Financial Plan, and design your own Investment Policy Statement. With those building blocks in hand, move forward in confidence, knowing that you can engage investment counsel and advice on your own terms, and evaluate their services objectively by holding them to the execution of your process constraints and achievement of your individual performance targets.

That puts you in control of the process with tools that perhaps you had not had the use of before. With a mind prepared to think about investing rationally rather than emotionally, your chances for investing successfully are improved.

Having read this far into this book, you have acquired concepts and tools that provide the potential to enhance your investing outcome if you choose to apply them in a businesslike discipline for thinking about investing. Warren Buffett repeatedly advises people that they would be better served by buying an index fund representing the S&P500 and I agree that for the 90% of investors that underperform the market returns, the index fund results would be an improvement. As an investor you need to decide if you are a defensive investor, or an enterprising investor as outlined by Graham who concluded *The Intelligent Investor* with a final chapter titled "Margin of Safety: The Central Concept." To sum up that final chapter, Graham said three things that readers would be well served to take to heart: *"Investment is most intelligent when it is most business-like...To achieve satisfactory investment results is easier than most people realize; to achieve superior results is harder than it looks."*

Chance favors the prepared mind.

—Louis Pasteur

APPENDICES

A: Successful Investing Fundamentals Checklist

B: Diversification

C: The Graham Formula

D: The Deals of the Dow©

E: Assessing the Graham Formula

F: The 3% Difference: Theory vs. Reality

G: Bibliography

H: Starter Tool Kit

I: Glossary

APPENDIX A

Successful Investing Fundamentals Checklist

Like the beacon of a lighthouse serves the sailor to navigate the path to safety and avoid treacherous hazards, the fundamentals for successful investing will guide the investor along the path to investment success through a framework for making rational financial decisions.

This appendix is provided to serve as a checklist of the component parts for that decision framework. It is that decision framework that serves as the investor's own illuminated guiding beacon to navigate their way to investment success.

The checklist has three parts: Part 1, Foundational; Part 2, Analytical; and Part 3, Confirmational.

The reader is reminded to keep in mind the caution of Bernard Baruch about the importance of making the efforts required:

The main reason why money is lost in stock speculation is not because Wall Street is dishonest, but because so many people persist in thinking that you can make money without working for it and that the stock exchange is the place where this miracle can be performed.

Part A: Foundational

1. A uniquely articulated Purpose (Statement of Objectives).
2. A clearly articulated Path to travel (Formal Financial Plan).
3. A defined Process to serve as a sound intellectual framework for making investment decisions (Investment Policy Statement).

Part B: Analytical

4. A small universe of quality investments, the "Dream Team".
5. Calculated Graham Formula estimates of intrinsic values.
6. The subset of qualifying margins of safety that exceed 33%.
7. Confirmation by analysis that the reason for the discount in valuation is but a temporary situation due to the market.
8. The identification of a "catalyst" for a repricing of valuation.

Part C: Confirmational

9. Support for your own analytical assessment confirmed by the opinion of a competent security analyst whose opinion you regard highly and in whom you have high confidence.
10. Insider trading activity that confirms the opportunity that you see supported by the closer knowledge of the business prospects that the management and directors of the organization possess.

APPENDIX B

Diversification

In 1970, William F. Sharpe authored *Portfolio Theory and Capital Markets,* published by McGraw Hill. He shared a Nobel Prize for his work on the Capital Markets Pricing Model (CAPM), which attempts to estimate the expected return of an investment based upon its Beta (volatility relative to the market) and the equity risk premium (the expected market return minus the risk-free rate). There are many issues of controversy around the CAPM that will not be addressed here. However, one item of his work from the Portfolio Theory text that was part of my Dalhousie MBA curriculum is his theory on diversification and the ideal size of a portfolio in terms of the number of securities required to optimize the benefits of diversification. It is elegantly summarized on page 150 of that text:

In sum, a little diversification can go a long way.

The basis for that conclusion is crucially important if you want to add value to your investing activities. In the real world of investment portfolios, most are grossly over-diversified, holding dozens and even hundreds of individual securities. To illustrate Sharpe's work, he built upon the work of John Evens, who derived a formula that shows how much volatility is reduced through diversification. That formula is:

$$\text{variability } (\sigma) = 11.91 + (8.63/n)$$

where n is the number of securities in the portfolio.

A major insight of Modern Portfolio Theory (MPT) is that a little diversification achieves a significant reduction in unsystematic ("specific company") portfolio risk. The following graph demonstrates the impact of diversification on volatility.

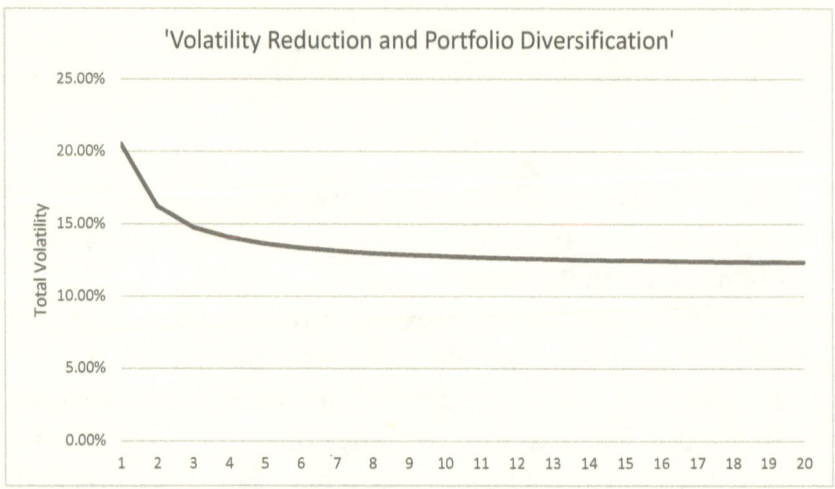

The marginal benefits of additional diversification are minuscule after the portfolio has eight to ten uncorrelated securities, and 85% of the benefit of diversification is achieved with a portfolio where N equals 5.

A portfolio of as few as eight to twelve issues that are not significantly correlated has approximately the same variability as the overall market. Systematic ("market") risk remains unaffected by the number of securities.

The majority of the benefits of diversification are achieved by a portfolio with only a few securities: "A typical equally weighted portfolio with ten securities will have only 7% more risk than the minimum possible, while one with twenty will have only 3% more than the minimum."[45]

---

45   William F. Sharpe, *Portfolio Theory and Capital Markets* (McGraw-Hill, 1970), p. 150.

After eight securities, the marginal benefit of reduced variability is less than 1% for each additional security in the portfolio, but the increased marginal risk from loss of focus is more than 10% with additional diversification (1/9 = 11%). Aside from the increased effort in following a larger number of securities (we all have our limitations), the critical element of FOCUS is diluted or lost, and the RISK of making errors in thinking is increased.

So, the section on diversification is concluded with a simple summary for those who want to add value through their efforts. Remember this:

You can't beat the market if you are the market.

To be able to see the mathematics in tabular format, the following page will demonstrate clearly how little benefit in variability is achieved with the addition of each new security into a portfolio.

After a portfolio has eight individual securities, the marginal reduction in variability by adding additional securities to the portfolio is less than 1%. Double the size of the portfolio to sixteen securities, and the variability declines from 12.99% to 12.45%. That is less than a 5% reduction (12.45/12.99 = 0.958). But the capacity of FOCUS has been reduced by 50%, so the quality of thought is significantly impaired. Thinking correctly is the key to successful investing.

The Investors' Advocate

The Sharpe Formula for Diversification in
Table Format of a Portfolio from One to Twenty Securities

Number of Securities	Total Volatility	Systematic (Market) Volatility	Security (Reducible) Volatility	Reduction in Total Volatility	Marginal Percentage Reduction	Cumulative Percentage Reduction
1	20.54%	11.91%	8.63%			
2	16.23%	11.91%	4.32%	4.32%	21.01%	21.01%
3	14.79%	11.91%	2.88%	1.44%	8.86%	28.01%
4	14.07%	11.91%	2.16%	0.72%	4.86%	31.51%
5	13.64%	11.91%	1.73%	0.43%	3.07%	33.61%
6	13.35%	11.91%	1.44%	0.29%	2.11%	35.01%
7	13.14%	11.91%	1.23%	0.21%	1.54%	36.01%
8	12.99%	11.91%	1.08%	0.15%	1.17%	36.76%
9	12.87%	11.91%	0.96%	0.12%	0.92%	37.35%
10	12.77%	11.91%	0.86%	0.10%	0.75%	37.81%
11	12.69%	11.91%	0.78%	0.08%	0.61%	38.20%
12	12.63%	11.91%	0.72%	0.07%	0.52%	38.51%
13	12.57%	11.91%	0.66%	0.06%	0.44%	38.78%
14	12.53%	11.91%	0.62%	0.05%	0.38%	39.01%
15	12.49%	11.91%	0.58%	0.04%	0.33%	39.21%
16	12.45%	11.91%	0.54%	0.04%	0.29%	39.39%
17	12.42%	11.91%	0.51%	0.03%	0.25%	39.54%
18	12.39%	11.91%	0.48%	0.03%	0.23%	39.68%
19	12.36%	11.91%	0.45%	0.03%	0.20%	39.80%
20	12.34%	11.91%	0.43%	0.02%	0.18%	39.91%

APPENDIX C

The Graham Formula

Benjamin Graham included this formula in his books *Security Analysis* and *The Intelligent Investor*. It represents a quick path to identifying an appropriate capitalization multiple for earnings. It does not produce an intrinsic value for any given earning stream. It does, however, attempt to provide a relative valuation for different companies' earnings that is dependent upon the rate of growth that the company is estimated to be able to maintain, adjusted for the interest-rate environment. Intrinsic value it is not, but it does provide a roughly comparable estimate between earning streams. What is significant about the way it functions is that it produces remarkable results in terms of performance when used as a valuation tool. Those results have worked for my practice, but they are independently assessed in the study that is referenced, "Assessing the Graham Formula: Too Good to Be True?"

In a company that had no earnings growth ($g = 0$) then the multiple would be 8.5 times. Where earnings grow at 5%, (a typical number for the overall market as measured by the S&P 500, the earnings multiple would be $(8.5+(2 \times 5)) = 18.5$ times, which is representative of the normal S&P 500 earnings multiple overall.

Value = Current (Normal) Earnings X $(8.5 + 2 \times g)$ where g is the expected annual growth rate in earnings per share.

For a more detailed discussion of the application refer to:

- Benjamin Graham, *Security Analysis*, 4th Edition. (New York: McGraw-Hill, 1951) pp. 536–538

- Benjamin Graham, *The Intelligent Investor*, fourth revised edition, (New York: Harper & Row Publishers Inc, 1973), p. 158.

- Open *Journal of Social Sciences*, 2014, 2, 1–5, "Assessing Graham's Formula for Stock Selection: Too Good to Be True?" Published online March 2014, in *Scientific Research*. http://www.scirp.org/journal/jss http://dx.doi.org/10.4236/jss.2014.23001

To quote the authors of the "Assessing Graham's Formula" study:

> Our findings related to Graham's formula's predictive power are quite remarkable. If starting before 1997, you selected companies to invest in based solely on Graham's formula and held the criteria that the companies must be trading at an RGV (relative Graham Value) below one with a margin of safety of 25%, you would have outperformed the Dow Jones Industrial Average in every year from 1997 to 2013, except for three years (1998, 2003, and 2011).
>
> In the portfolio where we took considerably more margin of safety at 50% (a market discount to Intrinsic Value of 33%), the results were even better. Graham's formula performed better than the DJIA in every single year. This phenomenal track record leads to the cumulative return over the DJIA in our second portfolio to be substantially higher, almost double that of our first portfolio.

The reader is reminded that in a few short years after the commencement of the period under study, the Internet bubble burst, resulting in significant declines in the market indices, especially the Nasdaq. Another event with similar results was the 9/11 attack on the United States' World Trade Towers and the Pentagon followed by multiple armed interventions in Iraq and Afghanistan. Yet, the Graham approach to investing through the formula as used in the referenced study to identify wide margins of safety (of 50%) in quality securities (selected from the DJIA 30 issues), produced cumulative annual returns more than two times those of the market without a single year of negative annual return.

Caveat Emptor: Limits of the Graham Formula

Readers are cautioned as to the limitations of the Graham Formula:

1. The Graham Formula does not derive the "intrinsic value" of an investment per se.
2. Rather, the formula provides a relatively uniform valuation estimate of individual securities for comparative purposes.
3. Those relative Graham Formula valuations provide the investor with several benefits:
   a) First, they serve as a place to efficiently focus one's efforts *for beginning the investment research and analysis process.*
   b) Second, that relative valuation is useful as a means of demonstrating the market's psychological enthusiasm or pessimism, both for a particular individual security and for the market in general, thereby providing the investor with the ability to stand apart from the crowd psychology (Mr. Market) in identifying potential candidates for investment.
   c) Third, they have served well in providing me with a measure of overall market risk reflected in collective valuation levels. When the collective DJIA 30 components' overall valuation *as a group*

approaches 80% (or higher) of the Graham Formula
values, history has repeatedly demonstrated that
the market is so near to being fully valued that
there is a significantly higher risk (because of that
smaller overall margin of safety) that the markets
will experience a correction. A higher level of
caution is advisable in the allocation of capital
and the exercise of patience is generally rewarded,
sometimes in short order as it was in early 2022.

4. Finally, if the ability to focus is indeed the key to
    business and investment success, the ultimate merits
    of the Graham Formula flow from quickly being
    able to eliminate those issues that do not qualify
    as relatively undervalued and allowing the user
    to then concentrate the efforts of detailed analysis
    on a smaller, more focused universe of candidates
    that demonstrate wide margins of safety.

No Magic Formulas

There is no magic formula that will provide an investor with
superior results. That goal is only derived from the diligent
exercise of good judgment. The Graham Formula is a tool for
focusing the efforts of the exercise of that judgment. Good
judgment comes from experience, most of it bad. Rather than
trying to exercise genius, lasting investment success flows from
rational decision-making and the avoidance of errors. In the
book titled *Winning the Loser's Game* by Charles Ellis, success
goes to those who make the fewest mistakes. That is true in
many endeavors (including investing), where unforced errors
often determine the outcome.

In J. Pierpont Morgan's terms, "Stocks will fluctuate."

Graham's *Security Analysis* opens with a quote from Horace: "Many shall be restored that are now fallen, and many shall fall that are now in honor."

The Graham Formula provides a means of identifying those individual stock-price fluctuations representing relatively wider margins of safety (opportunities for diligent analysis rather than direct investment).

From there, it is the investor's responsibility to perform the appropriate due diligence, the analysis to determine the cause and the nature (if temporary or permanent), and to identify if a potential catalyst might provide an expectation of the valuation being restored.

Graham's *The Intelligent Investor* opens with a quote from Aeneid: "Through chances various, through all vicissitudes, we make our way."

Graham's formula can be a tool to assist in converting vicissitudes into opportunities.

There are two notes that this author would make on the Graham Formula:

> First, the formula does not adjust for the impact of a company's dividend policy on its earnings growth rate. Back when Ben Graham developed this formula, the world was different: taxes were lower, and dividends were higher. Today, companies have moved towards buying back shares as partial compensation for the impact of taxes, so that in many companies, the dividend rate is half what it might have been decades earlier, but capital is also returned to shareholders through stock buybacks equivalent to the reduction of dividends.

> Second, this is problematic and can be demonstrated in a company that pays out all of its earnings as dividends. As a result, there is no reinvestment of earnings, no

accretion to shareholder capital, and hence, no growth in earnings. In the Graham formula, a company where there is no earnings growth (g = 0) is valued at a multiple of 8.5 times earnings. Take the same company and change the dividend policy to zero payouts, and the earnings then grow at the rate that the company uses those earnings to reduce its share count if it can invest the retained earnings profitably.

Consider a company that has the following structure:

Shareholder equity $100, represented by 100 shares outstanding, with a $1.00/share book value. Return on equity 15%, or after-tax earnings of $15.00, or $0.15/share.

Paid out as a dividend, there is no growth in book value and no growth in earnings. The formula values the shares to be worth 8.5 x $0.15 or $1.275, a small premium to the $1.00 book value per share.

Redirect the use of the earnings from paying dividends to buying back shares (at $1.275) and the resulting outstanding share count falls by 12 ($15.00/$1.275/share) to 88 shares and book value falls to $88.00.

The EPS jumps from $0.15 to $0.17 per share ($15/88), a growth rate of (.17/.15) 13.3%. Now the formula values the shares at (8.5 + (2 x 13.3)) a multiple of 35 times earnings or (35 x $0.17) = $5.95 per share.

That resulting formula calculation implies a valuation of the remaining 88 shares times $5.95 each or a total market capitalization of $523 - or 6 times the remaining $88 book value. That is a nonsensical jump in implied market capitalization of ($523/$127.5), 4.9 times the previous valuation as a no-growth company, simply because of a change from a 100% dividend payout policy to a 100% share buyback policy.

The formula has limitations.

My solution is simple. Recognize that the dividends were paid at the expense of growth. If you switched your holdings to an automatic dividend reinvestment program, you get the growth that would have been realized had the company bought back the shares. So, my version of how the formula might be amended to address the payout policy is to add the dividend yield (d) to the earnings growth rate (g): 8.5 + (2 x (g + d)), where g equals the earnings growth rate, and d equals the dividend yield.

Each earning stream is then evaluated uniformly, unaffected by differences in dividend policy. Examination of the result—i.e., which companies end up having the largest relative margins of safety—is little changed, although high-dividend payers get a small lift for what previously had been omitted from consideration.

Some notes for the reader to consider in the application of the formula for the real world of investment selection. An examination of the performance calculation numbers from the referenced Graham Formula study (see Appendix E) can conclude the following:

- The returns from investing in the Dow as an index saw $7,672 in 1997 grow to $14,875 in 2013 (seventeen years), representing a compound average growth rate (CAGR) of 4% *before considering dividends*. That would imply a market return somewhat shy of long-term averages but adding in dividends (the DJIA currently yields 2%) would serve to substantially close that index return vs total return gap.

- Applying the Graham Formula to invest only in Dow components the first scenario of using a 1.25 Relative Graham Value (RGV), (which translates to a discount from intrinsic value of 20% [(1/1.25) – 1=-.20]), the returns grow $7,672 to $32,861 equates to a CAGR of 9.5%.

- Finally, *and most importantly*, using the 1.50 RGV value scenario (or a discount to intrinsic value of 33.3% calculated as: [(1/1.5 = .667%) − 1 = -.333]. **That one-third discount to intrinsic value was (and remains) this portfolio manager's personal absolute minimum margin of safety.** The $7,672 initial investment value ends at $49,453. That value growth represents a CAGR of 12.4%. The result is effectively a 3% difference in annual return compared with the RGV of 1.25 above (12.4 − 9.5). That differential in return means a significantly larger result. To see just how important a small 3% difference in return can be, please examine "The 3% Difference" in Appendix F.

- In fact, in the seventeen years covered by the Graham Formula study, the ending capital sum is more than three times what the result would have been if invested in the Dow 30 as an index fund (when the RGV is 1.5, which is equivalent to a margin of safety of one-third or 33.3%).

$49,453/$14,975 = 3.3

Q.E.D.

APPENDIX D

The Deals of the Dow©

"The Deals of the Dow" is a proprietary version of the "Dogs of the Dow." Selected from the Dow 30 Industrial Index issuers are the ten stocks where the "margin of safety" is highest. In the "Dogs of the Dow," the ten issues with the highest dividend yields are selected. The example below is a snapshot of the "Deals" on April 13, 2023, using closing prices.

The Dow Jones Industrials Average as a group of thirty individual security issues, at the time of this snapshot of valuation, had a market price of $34,029.69. Intel, which in the spreadsheet has the largest discount to the Graham Formula valuation at 73.2, had fallen in price in recognition that returning to post-Covid normalcy would result in fewer desktop computers being sold and a reduced demand for Intel microprocessors as more people returned to work in their offices. The lower price also reflected significant competitive issues after years of mismanagement.

The point is that just because something registered as a discount to value does not prevent it from being repriced at an even larger discount. One needs to understand the reasons for the discount and then identify a catalyst that can change the perception of value and hence the pricing in the market. As research analysts' coverage of the issue begins to reflect the catalyst for change, the pricing of the issue on the market generally will reflect that more favorable research opinion coverage as it permeates the collective consensus of investor perception.

30 DOW JONES INDUSTRIAL AVERAGE ISSUES 14/04/2023

	ISSUER	SYMBOL	CLOSING PRICE	LTM EPS	TRAIL P/E	GRAHAM VALUE	MARGIN OF SAFETY	EARNING ESTIMATES		CAGR	YIELD
								NTM EPS	+4YR EPS		
1	3M	MMM	$106.15	$10.18	10.4	$224.40	52.7%	$11.50	$14.25	5.5%	5.8%
2	AMERICAN EXP.	AXP	$162.30	$10.02	16.2	$211.19	23.2%	$10.10	$12.85	6.2%	1.5%
3	AMGEN	AMGN	$251.44	$17.96	14.0	$353.89	29.0%	$17.85	$22.25	5.7%	3.4%
4	APPLE	AAPL	$165.56	$6.11	27.1	$159.02	-4.1%	$6.11	$8.55	8.8%	0.6%
5	BOEING	BA	$213.59	-$8.30	-25.7	$237.63	10.1%	$1.75	$12.55	63.6%	0.0%
6	CATERPILLAR	CAT	$221.67	$13.87	16.0	$290.84	23.8%	$15.20	$18.70	5.3%	2.2%
7	CHEVRON	CVX	$172.09	$18.28	9.4	$475.18	63.8%	$17.50	$25.00	9.3%	3.6%
8	CISCO	CSCO	$50.80	$3.36	15.1	$93.65	45.8%	$3.55	$5.00	8.9%	3.1%
9	COCA-COLA	KO	$63.15	$2.48	25.5	$59.80	-5.6%	$2.48	$3.35	7.8%	2.9%
10	DOW INC	DOW	$56.92	$8.98	6.3	$175.77	67.6%	$8.80	$11.00	5.7%	4.9%
11	GOLDMAN SACHS	GS	$332.13	$33.06	10.0	$977.27	66.0%	$34.00	$50.00	10.1%	3.0%
12	HOME DEPOT	HD	$292.15	$16.69	17.5	$173.99	-67.9%	$16.70	$17.35	1.0%	2.9%
13	HONEYWELL	HON	$195.90	$8.78	22.3	$318.42	38.5%	$8.75	$14.75	13.9%	2.2%
14	IBM	IBM	$127.90	$9.13	14.0	$176.92	27.7%	$9.15	$11.30	5.4%	5.1%
15	INTEL	INTC	$32.13	$1.85	17.4	$120.09	73.2%	$1.95	$5.00	26.5%	1.6%
16	JNJ	JNJ	$166.11	$10.16	16.3	$204.89	18.9%	$10.55	$13.05	5.5%	2.8%
17	JPMORGAN	JPM	$128.99	$12.09	10.7	$257.72	50.0%	$12.09	$15.50	6.4%	3.1%
18	MCDONALD'S	MCD	$289.07	$10.10	28.6	$251.37	-15.0%	$10.65	$14.25	7.6%	2.1%
19	MERCK	MRK	$115.58	$7.48	15.5	$137.13	15.7%	$7.40	$9.00	5.0%	2.6%
20	MICROSOFT	MSFT	$289.84	$9.21	31.5	$334.30	13.3%	$9.21	$15.50	13.9%	1.0%
21	NIKE	NKE	$126.43	$3.75	33.7	$202.13	37.5%	$3.75	$8.50	22.7%	1.1%
22	PROCTOR & GAMBLE	PG	$151.77	$5.81	26.1	$125.97	-20.5%	$5.81	$7.50	6.6%	2.5%
23	SALESFORCE	CRM	$194.02	$0.21	923.9	$89.84	-116.0%	$0.55	$5.45	77.4%	0.0%
24	TRAVELERS	TRV	$173.20	$11.09	15.6	$329.07	47.4%	$14.40	$19.00	7.2%	2.1%
25	UNITED HEALTH	UNH	$526.23	$22.19	23.7	$736.42	28.5%	$20.05	$34.00	14.1%	1.3%
26	VERIZON	VZ	$39.32	$5.18	7.6	$75.28	47.8%	$5.20	$5.85	3.0%	6.7%
27	VISA	V	$232.69	$7.50	31.0	$223.77	-4.0%	$7.50	$11.25	10.7%	0.8%
28	WALGREENS	WBA	$35.78	$5.04	7.1	$74.33	51.9%	$5.04	$5.70	3.1%	5.3%
29	WALMART	WMT	$149.49	$6.07	24.6	$175.46	14.8%	$5.85	$8.80	10.7%	1.5%
30	WALT DISNEY	DIS	$100.84	$1.75	57.6	$200.52	49.7%	$1.75	$9.60	53.0%	0.0%
	DOW JONES INDEX	34,030	$172.11	$9.00	19.1	$248.88	22.1%	$9.51	$13.83	14.4%	2.5%

The chart on the previous page of the Dow 30 Industrials with prices as of April 13, 2023, includes calculation of the comparative Benjamin Graham Formula Valuations (BGV). Note the wide divergence in P/E multiples and Graham Formula Valuation Discounts!

The following three subsets of ten issuers from the Dow 30 Industrials highlight the divergence in valuations:

The Dangers of the Dow

The ten highest priced issues within the Dow 30 based on the market price compared to the Graham Formula values.

THE DANGERS
(10 MOST EXPENSIVE GRAHAM VALUES)

	ISSUER	SYMBOL	PRICE	EPS	P/E	BGV	DISCOUNT	NTM EPS	+4YR EPS	CAGR	YIELD
1	SALESFORCE	CRM	$194.02	$0.21	923.9	$89.84	-116.0%	$0.55	$5.45	77.4%	0.0%
2	HOME DEPOT	HD	$292.15	$16.69	17.5	$173.99	-67.9%	$16.70	$17.35	1.0%	2.9%
3	PROCTOR & GAMBLE	PG	$151.77	$5.81	26.1	$125.97	-20.5%	$5.81	$7.50	6.6%	2.5%
4	MCDONALD'S	MCD	$289.07	$10.10	28.6	$251.37	-15.0%	$10.65	$14.25	7.6%	2.1%
5	COCA-COLA	KO	$63.15	$2.48	25.5	$59.80	-5.6%	$2.48	$3.35	7.8%	2.9%
6	VISA	V	$232.69	$7.50	31.0	$223.77	-4.0%	$7.50	$11.25	10.7%	0.8%
7	APPLE	AAPL	$165.56	$6.11	27.1	$159.02	-4.1%	$6.11	$8.55	8.8%	0.6%
8	BOEING	BA	$213.59	-$8.30	-25.7	$237.63	10.1%	$1.75	$12.55	63.6%	0.0%
9	WALMART	WMT	$149.49	$6.07	24.6	$175.46	14.8%	$5.85	$8.80	10.7%	1.5%
10	MICROSOFT	MSFT	$289.84	$9.21	31.5	$334.30	13.3%	$9.21	$15.50	13.9%	1.0%
			$204.13	$5.59	111.0	$183.12	-19.5%	$6.66	$10.46	20.8%	1.4%

The Dogs of the Dow

The ten issues with the highest dividend yields.

THE DOGS OF THE DOW
(10 HIGHEST DIVIDEND YIELDS)

	ISSUER	SYMBOL	LAST	EPS	P/E	BGV	DISCOUNT	NTM EPS	+4YR EPS	CAGR	YIELD
1	VERIZON	VZ	$39.32	$5.18	7.6	$75.28	47.8%	$5.20	$5.85	3.0%	6.7%
2	3M	MMM	$106.15	$10.18	10.4	$224.40	52.7%	$11.50	$14.25	5.5%	5.8%
3	WALGREENS	WBA	$35.78	$5.04	7.1	$74.33	51.9%	$5.04	$5.70	3.1%	5.3%
4	IBM	IBM	$127.90	$9.13	14.0	$176.92	27.7%	$9.15	$11.30	5.4%	5.1%
5	DOW INC	DOW	$56.92	$8.98	6.3	$175.77	67.6%	$8.80	$11.00	5.7%	4.9%
6	CHEVRON	CVX	$172.09	$18.28	9.4	$475.18	63.8%	$17.50	$25.00	9.3%	3.6%
7	AMGEN	AMGN	$251.44	$17.96	14.0	$353.89	29.0%	$17.85	$22.25	5.7%	3.4%
8	CISCO	CSCO	$50.80	$3.36	15.1	$93.65	45.8%	$3.55	$5.00	8.9%	3.1%
9	JPMORGAN	JPM	$128.99	$12.09	10.7	$257.72	50.0%	$12.09	$15.50	6.4%	3.1%
10	GOLDMAN SACHS	GS	$332.13	$33.06	10.0	$977.27	66.0%	$34.00	$50.00	10.1%	3.0%
			$130.15	$12.33	10.5	$288.44	50.2%	$12.47	$16.59	6.3%	4.4%

The Deals of the Dow

The ten issues with the largest discounts in market price relative to the Graham Formula values.

THE DEALS OF THE DOW
(10 LARGEST DISCOUNTS TO GRAHAM FORMULA VALUES)

	ISSUER	SYMBOL	LAST	EPS	P/E	BGV	DISCOUNT	NTM EPS	+4YR EPS	CAGR	YIELD
1	INTEL	INTC	$32.13	$1.85	17.4	$120.09	73.2%	$1.95	$5.00	26.5%	1.6%
2	DOW INC	DOW	$56.92	$8.98	6.3	$175.77	67.6%	$8.80	$11.00	5.7%	4.9%
3	GOLDMAN SACHS	GS	$332.13	$33.06	10.0	$977.27	66.0%	$34.00	$50.00	10.1%	3.0%
4	CHEVRON	CVX	$172.09	$18.28	9.4	$475.18	63.8%	$17.50	$25.00	9.3%	3.6%
5	3M	MMM	$106.15	$10.18	10.4	$224.40	52.7%	$11.50	$14.25	5.5%	5.8%
6	WALGREENS	WBA	$35.78	$5.04	7.1	$74.33	51.9%	$5.04	$5.70	3.1%	5.3%
7	JPMORGAN	JPM	$128.99	$12.09	10.7	$257.72	50.0%	$12.09	$15.50	6.4%	3.1%
8	WALT DISNEY	DIS	$100.84	$1.75	57.6	$200.52	49.7%	$1.75	$9.60	53.0%	0.0%
9	VERIZON	VZ	$39.32	$5.18	7.6	$75.28	47.8%	$5.20	$5.85	3.0%	6.7%
10	TRAVELERS	TRV	$173.20	$11.09	15.6	$329.07	47.4%	$14.40	$19.00	7.2%	2.1%
			$117.76	$10.75	15.2	$290.96	57.0%	$11.22	$16.09	13.0%	3.6%

As interest rates rise or decline, a safe assumption is that multiples will contract or expand. It is good to remember that equities, like bonds, are streams of future cash flows, except they are perpetual versions, as there is no fixed maturity date. And like bonds they are sensitive to changes in interest rates; the longer the maturity date (think duration), the greater the sensitivity. As equities have no maturity date, they are in effect equivalent to perpetual bonds.

The overall DJIA 30 issues have an average P/E of 19.1 and an average discount to Graham value of 22.1%. Taken as a whole, that is not unreasonable in historical terms. The issue here is an examination of how one can find opportunity that is more compelling.

The ten most expensive issues, as a group (the Dangers), have an average P/E of 111 times and an average price that is in excess of Graham value by 19.5%. The relative P/Es (111/19.1) indicate a premium in terms of a multiple of 5.8 times, while the compound annual growth rates (CAGR) of 20.8% for the Dangers vs. 14.4% for the overall DJIA indicates a premium in growth of 44%. That pricing of the optimism in the growth prospects results in an excess market value that provides a margin of safety that is less than zero (at −19.5%). As a result, the price in the market would indicate an optimistic investor sentiment with a significant risk of a contraction associated with a P/E multiple. In terms of the relationship to Graham's formula short form of intrinsic value, the ten Dangers are overvalued by 19.5%.

The ten Dogs of the Dow contain significant overlap with the ten Deals of the Dow in seven of ten issuers. The valuation discount (read margin of safety) is 50.2% for the Dogs compared with the Deals at 57%, again similar. The dividend yields at 4.4% and 3.6% do not represent a wide differential either. But in terms of growth of average earnings going forward, the Deals at 13% compared with the Dogs at 6.3% provide more than twice the earnings growth. And with the Deals, you get that at a margin of safety (57%) that is 13.5% greater.

For the ten Deals of the Dow, least expensive relative to the Graham Formula valuation at a 57% discount in value, at a P/E multiple of 15.2 times, the risk associated with a contraction is greatly reduced; the Deals' P/E multiple at 15.2 times is 79.6% of the entire Dow 30 as a whole (15.2/19.1=79.6%) and only 13.7% of the P/E multiple of the high-flying "Dangers of the Dow" group (15.2/111=13.7%).

Managing risk comes down to managing probabilities. In the present economic conditions of higher than targeted inflation, interest rates have risen, and for many companies, earnings multiples have contracted. In 2022 this was nowhere more so than for tech and growth companies.

Where P/E multiples and expectations are extremely low already, there are three options: expand, contract, or stay the same. Some companies might just defy the odds and expand.

Look for a catalyst and see where the insiders are putting their own capital.

The conclusion of this example, however, must address the single most important factor. While there is no absolute for intrinsic value, because it is an estimate and because change is constant, it is the relationship between market price to intrinsic value that powers the portfolio performance.

Buying dollars for dimes, or in this case for $0.43 does two things.

First, it provides the all-important **MARGIN OF SAFETY.**

Having a wide margin of safety protects capital, consistent with Buffett's two primary rules: Rule #1: "Never Lose Money"; Rule #2: "Never Forget Rule #1."[46]

Second, you make your money through the process of buying right.

If you buy right, there is little or no reason to ever sell, unless you are presented with superior opportunities. If you buy the shares of great businesses that will continue to reliably compound earnings into the distant future, you have an increased probability of a successful outcome.

But, if you came to make that investment at a price well below a reasonably conservative estimate of intrinsic value, then three of the most powerful forces in the investment universe: 1.) reversion to the mean, 2.) compound interest, and 3.) time, are all working in your favor.

A wide margin of safety not only protects capital from loss, it also significantly enhances returns and not just a little.

With those numbers serving as a conceptual guide to how you might apply the Graham Formula, Appendix E discusses a seventeen-year study of the relative performance attributed to that process.

---

46   Forbes 400, 27 October 1986; Janet C. Lowe Warren Buffett Speaks (1997)

APPENDIX E

Assessing the Graham Formula

In *The Intelligent Investor* by Benjamin Graham (1973), there is an appendix subtitled "The Superinvestors of Graham-and-Doddsville." That appendix by Warren Buffett is a transcript of a talk at Columbia University in 1984. That transcript begins with the following question:

"Is the Graham and Dodd "look for values with a significant margin of safety relative to prices" approach to security analysis out of date?"[47]

Buffett argues that it is not, despite the wide community of investment consensus to the contrary. He goes further to show it is not, with actual results of the followers of the approach.

Roll the calendar forward thirty years. In 2014, "Assessing the Graham Formula: Too Good to be True?" is published. In that paper, the "margin of safety" concept demonstrates the enduring intellectual value of the approach even when limited to a small thirty-stock sample universe of investment candidates comprising the Dow Jones Industrials Average.

So, there is a process that leads to a different result. That process has been demonstrated to produce extraordinary results over decades. It has worked for multiple investment stewards. The process has been shown to both function and endure; yet very few take advantage of it as a fundamental framework for making investment decisions.

---

47   The Intelligent Investor, Benjamin Graham, 4th Revised ed. p. 291 as an Appendix by Warren Buffett "The Super Investors of Graham-and-Doddsville,"

Recently Warren Buffett was interviewed regarding the investment results that are the driving force in Berkshire Hathaway's financial results.

If you look at the beginning of the Berkshire Hathaway annual report for fiscal 2021, its fifty-seven-year history (1965–2021) is shown. The per-share value is compared to the S&P 500 (with dividends reinvested).

The market returns for the S&P 500 averaged 10.5% annually.

The shares of Berkshire Hathaway averaged 20.1% annually.

Total cumulative returns:

S&P 500:   30,209%

Berkshire Hathaway: 3,641,613%

This led the interviewer to comment that even if Berkshire Hathaway shares fell by 99%, they would still have outperformed the S&P 500. Buffet's response: "Ben Graham would be proud. But let's not test the math."

Superinvestor of Graham-and-Doddsville, indeed.

The Proof Is in the Pudding

Lin, J. and Sung, J. (2014) "Assessing [the] Graham's Formula for Stock Selection: Too Good to Be True?" *Open Journal of Social Sciences*, **2**, 1-5.

http://dx.doi.org/10.4236/jss.2014.23001

Benjamin Graham offered a straightforward and simple formula to evaluate stocks' intrinsic value. Many regard the Graham Formula [as] a very simplistic way of estimating an individual company's intrinsic value. In this paper, we wanted to explore the effectiveness of Graham's formula. We wanted to see if using Graham's formula, investors can achieve excess returns above the market over a period of 17 years.

Included as a reference with the permission of the author, J. Lin

ASSESSING THE GRAHAM FORMULA RESULTS

		DOW JONES INDUSTRIAL AVERAGE	RELATIVE GRAHAM VALUE	
			RGV=1.25 PORTFOLIO	RGV=1.50 PORTFOLIO
STARTING YEAR	1997	$7,672	$7,672	$7,672
ENDING YEAR	2013	$14,975	$32,861	$49,453
MULTIPLE OF STARTING VALUE		1.95	4.28	6.45
COMPOUND ANNUAL GROWTH RATE (C.A.G.R.)		4.3%	9.5%	12.4%

NOTE: THE RELATIVE GRAHAM VALUE (RGV) OF 1.5 TIMES USED IN THE ASSESSING THE GRAHAM FORMULA STUDY IS EQUIVALENT TO A DISCOUNT FROM INTINSIC VALUE OF ONE THIRD (1/1.5=.667%). THAT DISCOUNT IS THE MINIMUM "MARGIN OF SAFETY" USED IN MY PRACTICE AS OUTLINED IN "T.I.P.S.: THE INTELLIGENT PORTFOLIO SOLUTION".

As a point of reference for the next section, Appendix F: "The 3% Difference—Theory vs Reality" and "Real World Differences in Rates of Compound Interest," it should be noted that the referenced study on the Graham Formula realized a value-added differential of return of 5.2% per year when the margin of safety was 20% (RGV = 1.25) and a much larger differential of 8.1% when the margin of safety (RGV = 1.5) was 33%.

Open Journal of Social Sciences, 2014, 2, 1-5
Published Online March 2014 in SciRes. http://www.scirp.org/journal/jss
http://dx.doi.org/10.4236/jss.2014.23001

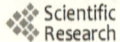
Scientific Research

Assessing the Graham's Formula for Stock Selection: Too Good to Be True?

Jason Lin[1], Jane Sung[2]

[1]Department of Business Administration, Truman State University, Kirksville, USA
[2]Department of Economics, Truman State University, Kirksville, USA
Email: jlin@truman.edu

Received October 2013

Abstract

Benjamin Graham offered a straightforward and simple formula to evaluate stocks' intrinsic value. Many regard the Graham Formula is a very simplistic way of measuring an individual company's intrinsic value. Graham and Warren Buffet however felt that the simplicity of the model allowed them to quickly and accurately identify undervalued companies, and stay away from overvalued ones. In this paper, we wanted to explore the effectiveness of the Graham's formula. We wanted to see if using the Graham's formula, investors can achieve excess returns above the market over a period of 17 years.

Keywords

Graham's Formula; Intrinsic Value

1. Introduction

Many regard the Graham Formula is a very simplistic way of measuring an individual company's intrinsic value. Graham and Warren Buffet however felt that the simplicity of the model allowed them to quickly and accurately identify undervalued companies, and stay away from overvalued ones. They understood that other strategies could produce excess returns, but that this strategy allowed them to do so with less risk. The formula was originally developed by economist Benjamin Graham in 1962 and was further revised by Mr. Graham in 1974 [1]. The formula requires two company specific inputs and one systematic input. The two company specific inputs are the company's earnings per share for the past twelve months and the company's long-term earnings growth estimate. The one systematic input is the yield on AAA corporate bonds. This allows the investor to take into account economic conditions that change the risk premium for low risk bonds, and the specific earnings and the growth of these earnings. Although usually described as the father of value investing, the formula can more accurately be described as G.A.R.P. or growth at a reasonable price because the higher the growth the more value the formula attributes to the stock.

While many view this method as far too simplistic to predict minor fluctuations in the market, the Graham Formula has been proven to be extremely useful in analyzing the stock market crash in October 1987. A study in the May-June 1988 Harvard Business Review titled "The Smart Crash of October 19th", the authors of the study,

How to cite this paper: Lin, J. and Sung, J. (2014) Assessing the Graham's Formula for Stock Selection: Too Good to Be True?
Open Journal of Social Sciences, **2**, 1-5. http://dx.doi.org/10.4236/jss.2014.23001

J. Lin, J. Sung

Arbel, Carvell, and Postnieks, (1988) [2] showed how remarkably well the Graham formula worked. The study showed that nearly all the stocks on the market were overvalued on October 1, 1987, using the Relative Graham Value (intrinsic value using Graham Formula divided by the current stock price). During the period preceding the crash many in the investing community talked about how the Graham formula was outdated and inconsistent with rational prices of the day. However, when the markets closed on October 19, 1987, the Relative Graham Value was remarkably close to one for a large majority of stocks listed on the exchange (Arbel, 1988). [2] The authors believed that instead of a burst of irrationality, the crash was a return to rationality when investors realized they couldn't make profits by buying overvalued securities and selling them at a higher price because eventually no one would pay that amount. During this period, the Graham formula was very accurate in predicting stock prices and the authors believe this is evidence that the Graham formula is a good tool for assigning value to a company's stock.

The authors of the study hypothesized that as the crash was happening, many investors went back to a fundamental approach of stock valuation, rather than the irrational exuberance that typified the 1980s stock market. This was made clear by the fact that a valuation technique such as the Graham Formula was so useful in explaining why stocks fell to the level they did. If the Graham formula was a good predictor of stock price, it would work best when markets were rational and there was no mispricing due to an over exuberance as the authors believed there was preceding the crash.

In this paper, we wanted to explore the effectiveness of the Graham's formula. We wanted to see if using the Graham's formula, investors can achieve excess returns above the market over a period of 17 years.

2. Literature Review

The Graham formula is a product of the 1930's market crash, and coming from those uncertain times, its goal was to "stand the test of the ever enigmatic future " as Graham himself mentioned in the preface to his book "Security Analyst" [3]. Graham developed his theory and elaborated on it in two of his most famous books, "Security Analyst" and "The Intelligent Investor". The main concept behind the formula is the belief that companies have an intrinsic value which the market doesn't necessarily reflect in their stock prices. The intrinsic value includes both tangible and intangible parts of the company and its determination is based on fundamental analysis rather than the stock price. Investor shouldn't be too concerned with the short term fluctuations in stock price, rather they should focus on the long run in order to achieve excess returns.

Benjamin Graham offered a straightforward and simple formula to evaluate stocks' intrinsic value. The formula consists of four inputs: current earnings per share, projected growth, the underlying appropriate earnings yield and interest expectations based on the AAA corporate bonds. This simplicity of the formula is in stark contrast to today's complex models, and perhaps because of its simplicity, it's often ignored in valuation methods and dismissed as too naive.

$$Value = \frac{EPS \times (8.5 + 2g) \times 4.4}{Y}$$

Using Graham's formula, a Relative Graham Value (RGV) is calculated by dividing the stock's intrinsic value by its current price [2]. It can be used to analyze whether a stock is undervalued or overvalued. If the RGV is above one, according to this theory the stock is undervalued and thus a good buy. On the contrary, if the RGV is below one the stock is overvalued and thus a good sell. The idea behind the Graham's formula however, goes against developments in more recent financial theory, most notably the efficient market hypothesis. Whereas the followers of the efficient market hypothesis believe that the market incorporates any new information into the stock prices, proponents of Graham argue that this is not the case. Using the Graham's formula, they believe that stocks can be underpriced and overpriced by the market and as such, there exist opportunities for returns in excess of the market. Most notable investors that follow Benjamin Graham's philosophy are Warren Buffett, John Bogle and Mario Gabelli. The ideas of Graham are not mainstream however, and as stated earlier, many dismiss the formula at too simple and not sophisticated enough.

3. Data and Methodology

To assess the predictive value of Graham's formula, we used the stock price and EPS of the 30 Blue Chip companies that compose the Dow Jones index [4]. The rule that we followed was that if the stock reached a RGV over our predetermined criterion, it would be bought and if the RGV went below it, it would be sold. Several assumptions were used in finding the input values for the Graham formulas:

1) The time period used in the comparison went from 1997 until 2013.

2) Diluted EPS of the 30 blue chip stocks was used.

3) Growth rate used was the annualized growth in EPS over the previous five years; to prevent negative stock prices, we limited the growth factor to −4.25% which would make $8.5 + 2 g = 0$.

4) For corporate bond rates, we used annualized yield based on monthly bond yields.

5) Stock prices and Dow Jones data were taken from the adjusted close on June 30th each year or the nearest previous trading day; furthermore stocks were adjusted for stock splits.

6) We checked to see if we needed to buy or sell stocks only on June 30th.

7) As the Dow Jones has changed composition, we followed suit; we only invested in stocks that were in the composite as of June 30th and divested of stocks that left the composite.

Furthermore, our analysis was split in two separate trials with RGV levels of 1.25 and 1.50 respectively. We bought the stock when its RGV was above the level and sold it when the RGV went below one. The portfolio was composed of equal market values of every stock invested in at the beginning of each year. Finally, for the purpose of this portfolio we liquidated our positions in 2013 regardless of the RGV.

We attempted to remove all sources of survivorship bias by using the current Dow Jones component companies for each year. We were able to find most of the companies still exist in one form or another but two stocks' data were hard to come by, AT & T before the merger with SBC and Union Carbide. In both of these cases, the company became a wholly owned subsidiary of another company and there is no currently traded stock that reflects their historical prices.

4. Results

Our findings related to Graham's formula's predictive power are quite remarkable. As stated before, we wanted to know whether or not Graham's formula could be used to achieve excess returns above the market as an investor. Benjamin Graham was a proponent of taking considerable margin of safety in investment decisions to allow for error in analysis and to provide for a stronger argument in favor of the same investment decision (Graham, 2006) [1]. For this reason, we assumed a position in the companies with RGV's greater than one at two different margins of safety levels. An RGV above one suggests that the company is currently underpriced in the market and should be bought, whereas an RGV below 1 suggests that the company is overvalued. With this in mind and to test the strength of Graham's formula, we assumed a portfolio that purchased into companies whenever their RGV was above one by a margin of safety of 25% and 50% (two separate trials) and sold the company's securities whenever their RGV fell below one. We felt that purchasing and selling at these respective levels was the best way to test the predictive power of Graham's formula because that is what it implied-an RGV above one means the company's stock is undervalued and an RGV below one means the company is overvalued. Again, what we found was pretty impressive.

If, starting before 1997, you selected companies to invest in based solely on Graham's formula and held the criteria that the companies must be trading at an RGV below one with a margin of safety of at 25%, you would have outperformed the Dow Jones Industrial Average in every year from 1997 to 2013 except for three years (1998, 2003, and 2011). The following **Table 1** shows our results with the first column being how much excess return Graham's formula was able to generate above the Dow Jones Industrial Average each year. The second column is measuring year over year, how much did the Graham's over perform the market on a cumulative basis. In the years that Graham's formula underperformed the market, it only underperformed marginally. When Graham's formula over performed the market, however, it did so substantially as we can see by 2013, the cumulative over performance by Graham's formula was 119.44% over the seventeen years.

For the portfolio where we took considerably more margin of safety at 50%, the results were even better. Graham's formula performed better than the DJIA in every single year. The second half of the **Table 1** summarizes our results for holding this portfolio. This phenomenal track record leads to the cumulative return over the DJIA in our second portfolio to be substantially higher, almost double that of our first portfolio.

If we look at the returns as a year over year compounded effect on total returns, we can see the difference in a measurable dollar amount. From 1997 to 2013, the Dow Jones Industrial Average went from 7672 to 14,975. If

J. Lin, J. Sung

Table 1. Summery of portfolio returns.

	Case I		Case II	
	Buy at RGV >= 1.25		Buy at RGV >= 1.5	
	Return over DJIA	Cumulative Return	Return over DJIA	Cumulative Return
1998	−1.57%	−1.57%	0.21%	0.21%
1999	4.95%	3.30%	5.05%	5.27%
2000	6.15%	9.66%	6.15%	11.74%
2001	19.95%	31.53%	22.05%	36.38%
2002	2.95%	35.41%	4.91%	43.08%
2003	−1.90%	32.84%	4.34%	49.29%
2004	6.71%	41.75%	19.47%	78.38%
2005	10.15%	56.14%	18.51%	111.37%
2006	3.05%	60.90%	6.74%	125.62%
2007	1.91%	63.98%	1.57%	129.16%
2008	7.01%	75.47%	6.94%	145.06%
2009	9.21%	91.63%	10.14%	169.91%
2010	5.21%	101.62%	6.15%	186.51%
2011	−1.64%	98.31%	1.47%	190.72%
2012	4.95%	108.13%	6.21%	208.78%
2013	5.44%	119.44%	6.95%	230.24%

we invested the amount of the DJIA index level ($7672) in 1997 in our portfolio guided by Graham's formula and purchased securities with RGV's greater than or equal to 1.25 while selling them when below 1, would end up as $32,861.14 at the end of June, 2013. If we invested $7672 in our portfolio as guided by Graham's formula and purchased securities with an RGV greater than or equal to 1.5 while selling them when below 1, our $7672 would be worth $49453.44 at the end of June, 2013. Bear in mind that this excludes any transaction costs associated with buying and selling as dictated by Graham's formula or fees associated with holding a mutual/index fund to mimic the DJIA portfolio. This is also under the assumption that our portfolio can only be revisited once per year, meaning we check the RGV level of our securities only on June 30th of each year. This means that our securities could be meeting our sell criterion sometime during the year before or after June 30th, and we would not have sold. The opposite case is also true-sometime during the year before or after June 30th the stock could have been meeting our buy criterion but we would not have bought. This represents a very illiquid portfolio which only adjusts its securities based on annual re-evaluation. It would have been interesting to see if Graham's formula could have outperformed or even underperformed the market more so if we allowed for monthly or even daily re-evaluation.

5. Concluding Remarks

We find Graham's formula mystifying in ways. One of the most simple valuation methods that we have ever seen produced by one of the most intelligent and distinguished minds in the history of finance. Even though the data that was presented to you suggests that Graham's formula can be actively used to outperform the market given a sufficient margin of safety, we are still hesitant moving forward to use this method as investors because of how worryingly simple it is. The formula does not ask for much and thus you're left feeling that you will not get much in return either. We feel this could be one of the main underlying reasons for the formula's success. No matter the evidence you present in favor of its predictive abilities, it likely is not used much if at all by insti-

J. Lin, J. Sung

tutional investors because of it perceived naivety. This could give the user of the formula an advantage. The market, a collection of all investors, determines stock prices at any given point in time. If this formula was used on a large scale by many investors the probability of outperforming the market would have to decline as prices reflect Graham's intrinsic value. Given that Graham's formula has been successful in retrospect and its usage is likely limited, this could provide potential for individual investors to do well in the markets. For those of us who do not have enough time to engage in individual security analysis and to keep up with the market, Graham's formula provides hope. Over the past seventeen years, using Graham's formula could have netted an investor more than double, in dollar amounts, what the Dow Jones Industrial Average would have netted them. Historical performance is never an indicator of future performance, but we have compelling evidence to suggest that there is some strength in this formula. Combined with further analysis and multiple other analyses the formula could provide an individual investors appreciable returns and ease of mind.

References

[1]   Arbel, A., Carvell, S. and Postnieks, E. (1988) The Smart Crash of October 19th. *Harvard Business Review*, 124-136.

[2]   Benjamin, G. (2013) Investopedia. http://www.investopedia.com/terms/b/bengraham.asp

[3]   Graham, B. (2006) The Intelligent Investor. Harper, New York.

[4]   Morningstar (2013) Morningstar Articles RSS.

APPENDIX F

The 3% Difference—Theory vs. Reality

"Theoretical" Difference of Compound Interest

The following forty-year tabular representation of compound interest shows two separate columns of a beginning capital sum of $100,000. One column compounds at 7%; another column compounds at 10%. The ending values after forty years are $1.5 and $4.5 million respectively.

What is demonstrated is the impact of a small 3% difference in return.

That 3% differential results in a terminal value that is three times larger because of 3% more in realized return. It matters not if the rate comparison is 4% vs. 7%, 7% vs. 10%, or 10% vs. 13%.

Over a forty-year investment horizon period, the ending terminal valuation is increased three-fold by the achievement of three extra percentage points of return. The point is simply this:

When it comes to compound interest, a few small extra points of return make a very large difference in the result over time.

THE 3% DIFFERENCE"©
THE DIFFERENCE 3% MAKES IN CUMULATIVE RETURN OVER 40 YEARS

YEARS	CAGR = 7% ACCOUNT	ROI		CAGR = 10% ACCOUNT	ROI		TERMINAL VALUE DIFFERENTIAL
0	$100,000	7.0%		$100,000	10.0%		$
1	$107,000	7.0%		$110,000	10.0%		$3,000
2	$114,490	7.0%		$121,000	10.0%		$6,510
3	$122,504	7.0%		$133,100	10.0%		$10,596
4	$131,080	7.0%		$146,410	10.0%		$15,330
5	$140,255	7.0%		$161,051	10.0%		$20,796
6	$150,073	7.0%		$177,156	10.0%		$27,083
7	$160,578	7.0%		$194,872	10.0%		$34,294
8	$171,819	7.0%		$214,359	10.0%		$42,540
9	$183,846	7.0%		$235,795	10.0%		$51,949
10	$196,715	7.0%		$259,374	10.0%		$62,659
11	$210,485	7.0%		$285,312	10.0%		$74,826
12	$225,219	7.0%		$313,843	10.0%		$88,624
13	$240,985	7.0%		$345,227	10.0%		$104,243
14	$257,853	7.0%		$379,750	10.0%		$121,896
15	$275,903	7.0%		$417,725	10.0%		$141,822
16	$295,216	7.0%		$459,497	10.0%		$164,281
17	$315,882	7.0%		$505,447	10.0%		$189,566
18	$337,993	7.0%		$555,992	10.0%		$217,999
19	$361,653	7.0%		$611,591	10.0%		$249,938
20	$386,968	7.0%		$672,750	10.0%		$285,782
21	$414,056	7.0%		$740,025	10.0%		$325,969
22	$443,040	7.0%		$814,027	10.0%		$370,987
23	$474,053	7.0%		$895,430	10.0%		$421,377
24	$507,237	7.0%		$984,973	10.0%		$477,737
25	$542,743	7.0%		$1,083,471	10.0%		$540,727
26	$580,735	7.0%		$1,191,818	10.0%		$611,082
27	$621,387	7.0%		$1,310,999	10.0%		$689,613
28	$664,884	7.0%		$1,442,099	10.0%		$777,216
29	$711,426	7.0%		$1,586,309	10.0%		$874,884
30	$761,226	7.0%		$1,744,940	10.0%		$983,715
31	$814,511	7.0%		$1,919,434	10.0%		$1,104,923
32	$871,527	7.0%		$2,111,378	10.0%		$1,239,851
33	$932,534	7.0%		$2,322,515	10.0%		$1,389,981
34	$997,811	7.0%		$2,554,767	10.0%		$1,556,956
35	$1,067,658	7.0%		$2,810,244	10.0%		$1,742,586
36	$1,142,394	7.0%		$3,091,268	10.0%		$1,948,874
37	$1,222,362	7.0%		$3,400,395	10.0%		$2,178,033
38	$1,307,927	7.0%		$3,740,434	10.0%		$2,432,507
39	$1,399,482	7.0%		$4,114,478	10.0%		$2,714,996
40	$1,497,446	7.0%		$4,525,926	10.0%		$3,028,480

"Real World" Differences in Rates of Compound Interest

The S&P 500 total return, 1985–2022, was 10.6%[48].

Fairfax Financial Holdings Stock Price Growth was 17.3%[49].

In the investment industry, Financial Plans attempt to establish conservative expectations.

> *Blessed be those of low expectations for they shall not be disappointed.*

A 7% expectation of total return is a frequently utilized target representing a balanced portfolio of bonds and stocks (40/60), where the bonds return 5% (5% x 40% = 2%) and stocks return 8.5% (8.5% x 60% = ~5%) for a total return of 7% (2% + 5% = 7%).

The actual return for the S&P 500 for the past thirty-seven years compounded at 10.6%. During that thirty-seven-year timeframe, the market price of the common shares Fairfax Financial Holdings compounded at 17.3%. The differential in terminal values of such a difference in compounded returns is shown in the table that follows.

For this example, $100,000 is used as the beginning account value. Invested to earn 10.6% in the S&P500 over thirty-seven years, it grows to $4.159 million. Invested at a rate of return of 17.3% like the share price of Fairfax Financial, it grows to be $32.487 million, an end result that is 7.8 times larger.

The 7.8 times differential demonstrates just how important the realization of extra return can be in the production of wealth. In this case, it was a 6.7% difference (rather than 3%) over the long term of thirty-seven years (1985–2022).

---

48   Fairfax Financial Holdings 2022 Annual Report page 21
49   Ibid.

RESULTS OF DIFFERENTIAL RATES OF RETURN

	S&P500			FAIRFAX FINANCIAL			RESULTING
	INDEX 37 YEAR			SHARE PRICE 37 YEAR			CUMMULATIVE
	CAGR = 10.6%			CAGR = 17.3%			DIFFERENTIAL
YEARS	ACCOUNT	ROI		ACCOUNT	ROI		
1985	$100,000	10.6%		$100,000	17.3%		$-
1986	$110,600	10.6%		$117,300	17.3%		$6,700
1987	$122,324	10.6%		$137,593	17.3%		$15,269
1988	$135,290	10.6%		$161,396	17.3%		$26,107
1989	$149,631	10.6%		$189,318	17.3%		$39,687
1990	$165,491	10.6%		$222,070	17.3%		$56,579
1991	$183,034	10.6%		$260,488	17.3%		$77,455
1992	$202,435	10.6%		$305,553	17.3%		$103,118
1993	$223,893	10.6%		$358,413	17.3%		$134,520
1994	$247,626	10.6%		$420,419	17.3%		$172,793
1995	$273,874	10.6%		$493,151	17.3%		$219,277
1996	$302,905	10.6%		$578,466	17.3%		$275,561
1997	$335,013	10.6%		$678,541	17.3%		$343,528
1998	$370,524	10.6%		$795,929	17.3%		$425,404
1999	$409,800	10.6%		$933,624	17.3%		$523,825
2000	$453,239	10.6%		$1,095,141	17.3%		$641,903
2001	$501,282	10.6%		$1,284,601	17.3%		$783,319
2002	$554,418	10.6%		$1,506,837	17.3%		$952,419
2003	$613,186	10.6%		$1,767,520	17.3%		$1,154,333
2004	$678,184	10.6%		$2,073,300	17.3%		$1,395,117
2005	$750,071	10.6%		$2,431,981	17.3%		$1,681,910
2006	$829,579	10.6%		$2,852,714	17.3%		$2,023,135
2007	$917,514	10.6%		$3,346,234	17.3%		$2,428,719
2008	$1,014,771	10.6%		$3,925,132	17.3%		$2,910,361
2009	$1,122,336	10.6%		$4,604,180	17.3%		$3,481,844
2010	$1,241,304	10.6%		$5,400,703	17.3%		$4,159,399
2011	$1,372,882	10.6%		$6,335,025	17.3%		$4,962,142
2012	$1,518,408	10.6%		$7,430,984	17.3%		$5,912,576
2013	$1,679,359	10.6%		$8,716,544	17.3%		$7,037,185
2014	$1,857,371	10.6%		$10,224,506	17.3%		$8,367,135
2015	$2,054,252	10.6%		$11,993,346	17.3%		$9,939,094
2016	$2,272,003	10.6%		$14,068,195	17.3%		$11,796,192
2017	$2,512,836	10.6%		$16,501,993	17.3%		$13,989,157
2018	$2,779,196	10.6%		$19,356,837	17.3%		$16,577,641
2019	$3,073,791	10.6%		$22,705,570	17.3%		$19,631,779
2020	$3,399,613	10.6%		$26,633,634	17.3%		$23,234,021
2021	$3,759,972	10.6%		$31,241,252	17.3%		$27,481,281
2022	$4,158,529	10.6%		$36,645,989	17.3%		$32,487,460

The real-world example of differential returns in the above chart is not a recommendation of Fairfax Financial Holdings. It is an example of what can be achieved through above average returns. Over the identical time period, the rate of returns in terms of compounding achieved by Berkshire Hathaway are nearly identical with those of Fairfax Financial, although on a significantly larger base. The returns are not actual. The average overall returns from the annual report are used here as examples of the power of compounding over time. A few extra points of return combined with a significant time period can have extraordinary results in creating value.

APPENDIX G

Bibliography

Baruch, Bernard M. *Baruch: My Own Story*. Toronto: Holt, Rinehart, 1957.

Bernstein, Peter L. *Against the Gods: The Remarkable Story of Risk*. New York: John Wiley & Sons, 1998.

Bevelin, Peter. *Seeking Wisdom, From Darwin to Munger*. Malmo, Sweden: Post Scriptum AB, 2007.

Bogle, John. Cf webinar hosted by the *Journal of Indexes* at www.indexuniverse.com.

Buffett, Warren E. *Berkshire Hathaway, Letters to the Shareholders*. *1965*

Caldini, Robert B. *Influence—The Psychology of Persuasion*. New York: William Morrow, 1993.

Fisher, Philip A. *Common Stocks, Uncommon Profits*. Hoboken NJ: John Wiley, 1996.

Graham, Benjamin and David Dodd. *Security Analysis*. New York: McGraw-Hill, 1951 (first published in 1934).

Graham, Benjamin. The Intelligent Investor, Benjamin Graham, fourth revised edition. New York: Harper & Row Publishers Inc, 1973. Appendix, "The Super Investors of Graham- and-Doddsville Appendix, Buffett, Warren E.

Graham, Benjamin. *The Intelligent Investor,* fourth revised edition. New York: Harper & Row, 1973.

Grant, James. *The Trouble with Prosperity*. New York: Times Books, Random House, Inc., 1996.

Keynes, John Maynard. *The General Theory of Employment, Interest, and Money,* New York, Harcourt Brace & World, Inc., 1965.

Lowenstein, Roger. *When Genius Failed: The Rise and Fall of Long-Term Capital Management.* New York: Random House, 2000.

Mackay, Charles (1814–1889), *Extraordinary Popular Delusions and the Madness of Crowds,* second edition. London: Office of the National Illustrated Library, 1852.

Sharpe, William F., *Portfolio Theory and Capital Markets.* USA: McGraw-Hill, 1970.

Siegel, Jeremy. *Stocks for the Long Run,* McGraw Hill.

Sullivan, Dan, *The Great Value Creator Escape, 2001, The Strategic Coach,* Toronto, Ontario.

Swensen, David F., *Pioneering Portfolio Management: An Unconventional Approach to Institutional Investment.* New York: Simon & Schuster Inc, 2000.

Trone, Donald B., *The Management of Investment Decisions,* Irwin, Chicago, 1996.

APPENDIX H

Starter Tool Kit

Available for Free:

Bloomberg—Futures, Commodities, and Currencies
https://www.bloomberg.com/markets/stocks/futures

Nasdaq Insider Activity
https://www.nasdaq.com/market-activity/quotes/
insider-activity

Value Line Dow 30 research reports
https://research.valueline.com/
research?=#list=dow30&sec=list

Warren Buffett on Value Line: "The snapshot it presents is an enormously efficient way for us to garner information about various businesses… I have yet to see a better way, including fooling around on the Internet, that gives me the information as quickly.

Yardeni Research—Updated Book Charts
https://www.yardeni.com/
https://twitter.com/yardeni?lang=en

Available by Subscription:

Barron's: https://barrons.com

Bloomberg: https://Bloomberg.com

Economist: https://www.economist.com/

Globe and Mail: Watch List/Reuters Stock Reports: https://
www.theglobeandmail.com/

Value Line Inc.: https://investors.valueline.com

Wall Street Journal: https://wsj.com

For a Better View

> *If I have seen further,*
> *it is by standing on the shoulders of giants.*
> —Sir Isaac Newton

Warren Buffett / Berkshire Hathaway

The Chairman's Messages
https://www.berkshirehathaway.com/letters/letters.html

The Track Record
https://www.berkshirehathaway.com/2021ar/2021ar.pdf

Prem Watsa / Fairfax Financial Holdings

Shareholder Letter
https://s1.q4cdn.com/579586326/files/doc_financials/2021/FF/Fairfax-Financial's-Shareholders'-Letter-2021-(with-attachments).pdf

The Track Record
https://s1.q4cdn.com/579586326/files/doc_financials/2021/FF/WEBSITE-Fairfax-Financial's-2021-Annual-Report.pdf

APPENDIX I

Glossary

Alpha

Excess return earned over a benchmark adjusted for risk attributable to investment management value added.

Asset Allocation

Making the decision to deploy resources (both financial and human) to best achieve the results they are capable of producing. In Graham's teachings, the investor divides their capital in two parts. One half is allocated to equities; the other is deployed between equities or fixed income, depending upon the investor's assessment of the most attractive risk-adjusted opportunity at the time.

Jacob de Rich (nee Jacob Fugger) advised dividing assets into four equal pools: coin (cash), receivables (bonds), gold, and real estate and rebalancing once each year. The appropriate allocation of assets is dependent on an individual's abilities, objectives, and risk tolerance within the context of market conditions.

Capitalization of Future Earnings

The Graham Formula is one means of valuing a future earnings stream dependent upon growth in those earnings and the interest-rate environment. In real estate, the capitalization of net rental incomes is arrived at within a market context by dividing the income by a hurdle rate, net rent/interest rate=capitalized value. W.F. Sharpe was awarded a Noble Prize for his work on modern portfolio theory (MPT) and his capital-asset pricing model (CAPM). For example, the capitalized value of an earnings stream is the result of dividing it by a minimum return expectation of 15%; $1 earnings/15%=$6.67

Commissioned-based investment advisory business,

Commission revenue is the underlying motivational incentive of the sales-agency relationship. It presents an inherent conflict of interest between those of the salesman and of the client. Behavior follows incentive; compensate on trading and the trading activity will be the motivation for the relationship. This is not possible for a fiduciary acting in the best interest of the client.

Compound Average Growth Rate (CAGR)

The rate at which a capital sum compounds in value over a given period of time. Consider the "Rule of 72" as a shorthand method of determining the interest rate required to double a capital sum within a specified period of time: $1 becomes $2 in 7.2 years if it compounds at 10% (72 divided by 10 as the interest rate yields 7.2 years). Google "Rule of 72" for more information.

Defensive investor

In Graham terms, a defensive investor is loss averse and seeking freedom from effort in the need for frequent decisions.

Discounted Cash Flow Analysis (DCF)

A mathematical means of determining the present value of a future earnings stream using a discount rate to adjust the cash flows due in future periods into what they are worth to a buyer today.

Diversification

The process of adding investments to a portfolio in order to reduce specific company risk. Specific company risk can be substantially reduced by 80% to 90% through diversification. The benefits of this can be achieved by holding five to eight uncorrelated securities. The complement to portfolio risk, known as systematic risk or otherwise referred to as market risk, is not able to be reduced by diversification of holdings. To achieve that benefit, see asset allocation. Holding more than ten securities in a portfolio achieves little benefit in respect to risk management; each additional holding increases the risk that your focus on the portfolio will be diluted and that you will make mistakes. Excess diversification is a form of what Peter Lynch coined "Diworsification": the process of adding investments to a portfolio in such a way that the risk/return trade-off is made worse.

Enterprising Investor

The enterprising (active or aggressive) investor is willing to devote time and effort to select securities more attractive than average.

Equity Risk Premium

The premium in terms of interest (or discount) rate is required to equate earnings that are uncertain in their timing and risk (from equity investments that fluctuate due to the vicissitudes of market uncertainty) to the less uncertain earnings that can be expected from the covenants of bonds and fixed income with stated maturity dates. In longer periods of time, the equity-risk premium is shown to be the total return of the stock market (8–10%) compared to the bonds market (~6%). Returns of 9% equity divided by 6% bond returns equals an equity-risk premium of 1.5 times or 50% more return related to the increased risk and volatility of equities compared to bonds.

Fee-Based Investment Advisory Business

This is the business model of the fiduciary. The advisor is compensated by a fee as a percentage of assets under management, performance, or a combination. As the client is successful, so is the advisor. There is no incentive to generate commissions on the basis of trading activity because there are no commissions.

Fiduciary

A fiduciary is a person acting in the interest of others with the characteristics of a trustee. When acting in the fiduciary role in the management of money or assets for others, the fiduciary is obligated to put their client's interest first and act in the interests of their client with scrupulous good faith and candor, not in their own interest.

Forward Earnings

Usually the expected next twelve months (NTM) of earnings.

Growth Rate in Earnings

The growth rate in earnings expected to be achieved over a period of years. Here the most important question is: What is the "sustainable" earnings growth rate able to be achieved by an enterprise because of durable competitive advantages (which may deteriorate over time)? If a company realizes $1 in earnings, after both the allowances for ongoing capital expenditures to maintain physical plant and equipment and the payment of dividends, on an equity basis of $10, then the math would indicate a potential growth rate of 10%, representing the growth in capital subject to opportunities to expand the business and competitive, technological, and other threats.

Intrinsic Value

The measure of an asset's present worth based upon the present value of future cash flows. Over long periods of time, the market value and intrinsic value of an investment tend to be similar, but in short-term periods, market prices and intrinsic values can be widely divergent due to issues of perception by market participants.

Investment Horizon

The period of time over which an investment is contemplated being owned or the period of time that the financial plans encompass.

Investment Return

The total of returns realized (interest, dividends, capital gains/losses) as a percentage of the investment's costs.

Investor Return

The realized returns of the investor, which often differ from the actual returns of the investment, due to issues around the timing of the acquisition and divestiture. When buying and holding for long periods, investment and investor returns are equivalent except for fees and transaction costs. In shorter periods, the investor generally underperforms the investment due to human behavioral issues. See DALBAR reports on this subject. Also see actual realized returns by successful investors like Warren Buffett and Prem Watsa.

Management of Probabilities

Understanding the inputs to risk and opportunity is key to management of probability in investing. Balance-sheet risk can be a path to insolvency, but balance-sheet strength can be a durable competitive advantage. Management character is a means of protecting the investor from unscrupulous malfeasance in the corporation and is the investor's most important tool for reducing risk and for realizing opportunity. Buying investments of quality when they are available at wide discounts to intrinsic value is the single best risk protection and also the driver of enhanced returns. The list of factors goes on beyond the scope of this book, but the single biggest risk faced by the investor is the investor's own emotions. Managing this probability of error is best achieved through having an articulated process (an investment policy statement) tailored to the investor's personal priorities (Statement of Investment Objectives and Financial Plan).

Management of Risk

Determine (1) the margin of safety that the current market price represents as a discount from intrinsic value, (2) if the reason for the discount is one of a temporary nature or (3) due to a permanent impairment of the business enterprise, (4) identify a catalyst that may result in the repricing of the investment to recognize the underlying intrinsic value, (5) have the courage to act upon your convictions and, (6) maintain the temperament of character to have the patience for the events to unfold.

Margin of Safety

The difference between an investment's market price and intrinsic value. Combined with temperament, the margin of safety provides an investor with a significant advantage to realize returns that are superior to the norm.

Market Interest Rates

Interest rates change over time, due to many factors. Inflationary expectations, central bank interventions, and geopolitics are but three. There are different rates in the term structure of markets, for example: variable-rate vs. fixed-rate mortgages (maturity risk), short-term or long-term bonds (duration risk), and credit ratings (default risk).

Modern Portfolio Theory (MPT)

Attributed to the Noble laureate Harry Markowitz in a 1952 publication titled *Portfolio Selection*, using diversification and asset allocation to optimize expected return relative to volatility along an "efficient frontier" optimizing return for a given level of risk. It assumes markets are efficient and that all information is readily known about a given security, which is in direct conflict with the basic tenets of value investing based on capitalizing on inefficiencies or mispricing of securities relative to intrinsic values.

Net Cash Flow

The earnings from a business with non-cash charges (depreciation and amortization) added, minus capital expenditures undertaken to maintain existing production capacity and build for future expansion.

Opportunity

In investing, opportunity is presented where the investor can deploy resources to acquire an asset at a price that will provide security of principal and an adequate return. Anything else is speculation and that is the equivalent of risk of loss and adverse outcomes.

Price Earnings Ratio

Commonly abbreviated as P/E on a per share basis where the P represents "Price," and the E represents "Earnings."

Probability

The likelihood of an outcome, often statistically measured in standard deviations from the mean. In simple terms, the number of favorable outcomes divided by the total number of possible outcomes. Human nature in investing tends to overestimate the probability of favorable outcomes and underestimate the risk of the unfavorable. Hence the reliance on "a system" by gamblers, whether it be statistically valid or not.

Regression Analysis

Fitting an independent variable to a dependent variable using least squares analysis. The Graham Formula ($Y = 8.5 + (2 \times G)$) is an example of an attempt to "fit" the valuation multiple (Y) as a dependent variable to be used to capitalize a series of earnings to a function of a constant (8.5) plus an independent variable representing the growth rate in earnings (G).

Reported Earnings

The reported earnings figure is statutorily required for public companies on a regular audited basis to maintain the qualification for listings with various exchanges. Generally Accepted Accounting Principles (GAAP) specify the parameters of what are to be used in arriving at the earnings figure. There remain wide areas of interpretation within the application of GAAP principles.

Risk Management

If risk is the effect of uncertainty on objectives, management of those risks involves identifying, evaluating, and prioritizing those risks. Negative, unfavorable events are seen as risks. Positive events and outcomes are opportunities.

Risk vs. Volatility

In modern investment finance, volatility is improperly equated with risk. Volatility is an investor's best friend for it is where opportunity is found as the conditions present the investor with the ability to acquire investments for less than they are really (intrinsically) worth. Risk is the chance, probability, or possibility of an unanticipated outcome that may result in loss. Risk is what happens "when you do not know what you are doing"[50] in Warren Buffett's terms. In insurance underwriting, risk is what you address by spreading loss from one who experiences it among many who insure against it using underwriting (premiums).

Standard Deviation

Standard deviation is a statistical measure of the amount of variation or dispersion from the mean of a set of observed values within a data set. Typically associated graphically with a bell curve, the measure of standard deviation is calculated using the sum of the squares of deviations from the mean methodology.

Terminal Capital Value

The estimated value of an asset at the end of a forecast period. It is used as part of the calculation to estimate the value of a stream of cash flows over the forecast period and typically in estimating the cost of capital or the internal rate of return of a project's profitability in a discounted cash flow (DCF) analysis.

Valuation

Process of analysis to assess the worth of an asset, usually performed from a multiple of techniques: public market value,

---

50   1994 January 2, Omaha World Herald, Jim Rasmussen quoting Buffett speaking to Columbia University students, supra.

intrinsic value, discounted cash-flow value, private-market value, and the list goes on.

Value Line

An independent investment research and financial publishing firm based in New York. Its name is taken from the "value line" that the firm calculates for the companies it follows, where it attempts to fit a form of least squares regression line to model the stock price of covered investment issuers to an underlying variable—typically earnings, cash flow, or dividends.

Variability

A term used to describe the measure of distance of individual data points from a mean value of the data set.

Variation

A change or difference in condition, measured within certain limits.

Volatility

Although often equated with risk, volatility is not risk. Volatility is fluctuation, change, and variability. Unfavorable volatility that impacts outcomes adversely represents one measure of risk; while the opposite side of volatility, which favorably impacts outcomes, represents opportunity.

ABOUT THE AUTHOR

Payson Y. Hunter has over forty years of experience in financial management, including twenty-five years as a discretionary portfolio manager. As a fiduciary responsible for the welfare of hundreds of clients and hundreds of millions of dollars in assets, he has carried those responsibilities without a single client complaint. In addition to having a B.A. in Political Science and Economics from Kent State University, and a B.Comm. and an M.B.A. from Dalhousie University, he is a Certified Public Accountant, a Chartered Accountant, and a Certified Investment Manager. Happiest when helping people to create value, he wrote *The Investors' Advocate* to help people achieve their objectives.

www.ingramcontent.com/pod-product-compliance
Lightning Source LLC
Chambersburg PA
CBHW030928180526
45163CB00002B/501